The Puritan Imagination

The Puritan Imagination

Bishop Joseph Hall's Use of Meditation

TODD D. BAUCUM

WIPF & STOCK · Eugene, Oregon

THE PURITAN IMAGINATION
Bishop Joseph Hall's Use of Meditation

Copyright © 2022 Todd D. Baucum. All rights reserved. Except for brief quotations in critical publications or reviews, no part of this book may be reproduced in any manner without prior written permission from the publisher. Write: Permissions, Wipf and Stock Publishers, 199 W. 8th Ave., Suite 3, Eugene, OR 97401.

Wipf & Stock
An Imprint of Wipf and Stock Publishers
199 W. 8th Ave., Suite 3
Eugene, OR 97401

www.wipfandstock.com

PAPERBACK ISBN: 978-1-6667-3545-1
HARDCOVER ISBN: 978-1-6667-9254-6
EBOOK ISBN: 978-1-6667-9255-3

Scripture quotations from The Authorized (King James) Version. Rights in the Authorized Version in the United Kingdom are vested in the Crown. Reproduced by permission of the Crown's patentee, Cambridge University Press

Scripture quotations taken from the Amplified® Bible (AMP), Copyright © 2015 by The Lockman Foundation. Used by permission. www.lockman.org

07/28/22

To the memory of Sister George Towle and in recognition
of the Sisters of Charity in Leavenworth, Kansas.

Contents

Preface | ix

Acknowledgments | xiii

Introduction | 1

Chapter 1: Recovering the Practice of Meditation | 9

Chapter 2: A Puritan Primer in Reformed Devotion | 27

Chapter 3: *The Art of Meditation*: Analysis | 38

Chapter 4: *The Art of Divine Meditation* Compared | 78

Chapter 5: Hall's Use of Tradition on the Soul and its Faculties | 97

Chapter 6: Occasional Meditation and the Puritan Imagination | 119

Appendix A: Hall's Sources Overview | 135

Appendix B: Timeline of Bishop Hall | 137

Appendix C: Steps of Meditation Illustrated | 139

Bibliography | 141

Preface

The sweetest thing in all my life has been the longing—to reach the Mountain, to find the place where all the beauty came from—my country, the place where I ought to have been born. Do you think it all meant nothing, all the longing? The longing for home?[1]

THIS BOOK REFLECTS A personal reason for being drawn to the work of Bishop Hall, a moderate churchman at the Norwich Cathedral during the English Civil War. For I have found a writer whose soul and own times were out of step, indeed even hostile to his conciliar approach to faithful love of God and the historic continuity of a community of faith rooted back to the early church. I write as a Presbyterian with a high regard for the church, but a church divided by warring parties. Hall revealed in his life that love of God has a particular outworking in the sphere of the saints. Simply stated, it should follow that loving Christ should make one love his bride, which on earth is the "one, holy, catholic, and apostolic church." The times we live in, to my way of thinking, are neither congenial to such a temperament nor broadly receptive to a balanced conception of living out a biblical and historical expression of Christianity.[2] Too often purity of faith is rooted in sectarian attitudes that do little to honor the legacy of some of the Puritans, who, like Hall, valued both orthodox doctrine and the unity of the church. When schism is lightly embraced over purity, or orthodoxy is weaponized for ideological purposes, something vital is lost. Yet, commitment to core and apostolic faith need not be squandered in maintaining unity. Indeed, the life and witness of Bishop Hall reveals that often the cost borne in such

---

1. C. S. Lewis, *Till We Have Faces*, 75.
2. John Stott, *Balanced Christianity*.

an unpopular position is deeply personal. Still even more importantly, Hall knew the remedy for this conflict was not better arguments, but a deeper and richer relationship with Christ.

Secondly, my first exposure to the practice of meditation was through taking martial arts as a high school student. Years later, during my first years in ministry, I went on retreats using resources from Roman Catholic writers on meditation and contemplation. The sisters at the motherhouse of the Sisters of Charity in Leavenworth, Kansas, were my guides, especially Sister George, my spiritual grandmother. We met when I was serving my first pastorate in Kansas. Our first daughter, who was four at the time, would, because of her black habit with its white and black headcover, refer to her as "the Jesus lady." The name was more accurate than we understood at the time. She introduced me to using my imagination to read the Scriptures along with Ignatius. After decades as a pastor, it was my discovery of the Puritans that has brought me a renewed understanding of the Christian practice of meditation, often neglected by us left-brain Protestants. After serving in both mainline and evangelical churches, I've seen the danger of this binary, either/or spirit of the age that has malnourished our churches and our spiritual health. Evangelicals tend to emphasize the rational part of the faith, often to the detriment of fully appreciating the noncognitive part of the human soul called the subconscious. Because the founder of the school of psychoanalysis, Sigmund Freud, was an atheist, we are often distrustful of the psychology of the soul, and much of what Freud wrote about the subconscious. But Freud's dismissal of religion aside, the Bible speaks about the soul and the human dialogue with the heart, long before the Swiss doctor thought of psychoanalysis as a way to plumb the unconscious, troubled minds of his patients in Vienna. We need to recover the importance of the unconscious or the pre-cognitive imagination of the soul that forms so much of who we are and what we do.

Hall understood that meditation fans the flame of love for God. It changes our hearts and enlarges our soul with the reality of God. It enables the gospel of grace (which is more than an idea) to restructure and reformulate our understanding—our brains/psyche—along new ways of thinking and being. The message of this grace, which is the truth of Jesus (we are justified by faith)—has the power to change us in the inner complexity of our soul—the non-thinking, the precognitive; the where we go when we are just there, before we think, before we speak, and before we act, or what Scriptures call the "inner spring of the heart" (John 7:38). This is a picture of the soul. This is the true self, our inner life. Meditation is God's avenue towards the heart to make us holy—towards a movement in the way of truly knowing and loving God. Meditation is a key to letting the truth of the gospel permeate every aspect of our being, our thinking, our emotions, our heart, and our daily lives.³

Bishop Hall's model of meditation was his life's tribute and legacy to his, and I pray our, divided times. His invitation to climb the mountain of closer communion with Jesus is perhaps the greatest word one can heed; both personally and, by God's grace, collectively, may we heed his example, for our social and inward integrity as Christians in our divided contemporary times.

---

3. Phil 4:8: "Finally, *brothers and sisters*, whatsoever things are true, whatsoever things *are* honest, whatsoever things *are* just, whatsoever things *are* pure, whatsoever things *are* lovely, whatsoever things *are* of good report; if *there be* any virtue, and if *there be* any praise, think (*logozami*) on these things" (emphasis added).

Acknowledgments

A BOOK HAS A hidden story of many people shaping, acting as mid-wives behind the scenes, the time when it is to be read by others. It is only right to mention some of the people who helped me in this project. Dr. Greg Salazar, my advisor in the original thesis form, was unselfish in giving it a multitude of readings and pushing me to rethink sections or to clarify obscure points. The errors and obscurity that remain are my own. Overall, he encouraged me in the effort to bring to light such a neglected star among celebrated writers of the Puritan era. Years ago, in my study at Trinity School for Ministry, I experienced how valuable Anglican spirituality would be to my own journey and of course J.I. Packer's love for the Puritans helped me get acquainted with this part of mystical theology. My first encounter with the need to balance piety and orthodoxy was taking church history and doctrine at Memphis Theological Seminary with Dr. "Knick" Knickerbocker, who became for several of us at that time, the "great Knick." His unique bridge between the past and present and personal example of leaving academics to serve as a parish priest in the Catholic church, speaks to the life of Bishop Hall, a man of deep piety and love for both God and the world. Finally, and with heartfelt gratitude, I thank my wife Mary for her encouragement, faith in me and patience in the years that this book was born.

Introduction

It is Thou only that canst turn away mine eyes from regarding these follies and my heart from affecting them. Thou only, who as Thou shalt one day receive my soul in heaven, so now before-hand canst fix my soul upon heaven and Thee.[1]

THIS WORK SETS FORTH the claim that Bishop Joseph Hall is a foundational author and whose work on meditation in general provided the basis for claiming him as a key promoter of Protestant asceticism in the seventeenth century. It will argue that the balanced approach to the imagination and the rational part of the soul was the contribution that Hall made on the literature of meditation, drawing upon an Augustinian understanding of human faculties and other patristics. Yet, the question can be asked: If Hall was such a key source for a Protestant approach to meditation and piety, why is he not well known or referenced as other writers or held in high esteem? It is a question worth pondering for a contemporary evaluation as a historical study. How might a foundational author be neglected? This may be due for various reasons. The polemics of seventeenth-century England became more partisan after the Restoration, when the son of Charles I, publicly executed by Parliament, took back the throne. Scholars using Thomas Hooker or Hall or even Ussher in the eighteenth and nineteenth century often had a bias towards one set of opinions of theology.[2] Bias is one aspect; secondly,

---

1. Hall, *Art*, 103.
2. MacCulloch, *All Things Made New*, 318. He notes how one bias would view central dogmas to the Reformation: "Henry Fish, in his diatribe *Jesuitism*, traced in the movements of the Oxford Tractarians, criticized E. B. Pusey, the doyen of the Oxford Movement, for citing Hooker and Andrewes 'in confirmation of Mr. Newman's views of Justification: whereas the views of both those men were the very reverse of Mr.

while Hall was known and read into the eighteenth century, there was also a revival of some of his works in the nineteenth century. For about a century, Joseph Hall has not been of great interest from a theological vantage point. Sporadic interests have been in literary circles, as noted by Martz, Kauffman, and Huntley; all literary specialists in seventeenth-century British literature.

Studies involving in-depth research in the complex and scholarly work of the Puritans and their cultural milieu is recovering a sense of new appreciation of this movement and period, clearing away a bias that misunderstood their views and their positive contribution to the church at large. Hall was a man who defies easy labels and yet represented the core of Reformed faith extolled at the Synod of Dordt, albeit a moderate in his views of the church in a contentious time of ecclesiastical debates. His work on meditation was intentionally written to cultivate deeper spiritual practices within the tradition of his own church even as Counter-Reformation trends were working to win Protestants back to Rome through piety and polemics, whether by carrots or sticks. Hall did not write to establish an English order of spiritual soldiers; there is no indication of hubris or vanity in his writings, where the primary virtue he extolled was humility, just like the Augustinians he emulated. He laid a foundation of thinking about the role of the imagination and how the taxonomy of meditation can be understood contextually in the seventeenth century. The ongoing debate about the positive and negative use of the imagination is vitally important to affirm Hall's contribution within a trajectory of Reformed orthodoxy, even with the variety of views that were held among Protestants of that era.

The claiming of the term "Reformed Contemplative" is defended in the context of retrieval and continuity with contemplative practices fostered in medieval and patristic monasticism that balanced prayer and work, solitude and service, and importantly ascetical theology that emphasized the heart without ignoring the rational mind. Meditation cultivates the heart for greater love of God rather than a theory of God. Jean Gerson defined mysticism as "outreach of the soul to a union with God through the desire of love, which resides not within the intellect but in the affective power of the soul."[3] This use of ascetical piety often employed the language of scales and progressive steps in pursuing deeper union with Christ, as the calling for every Christian in the joyful task of holiness.

> How far off is yonder great mountain! My very eye is weary with the foresight of so great a distance, yet time and patience shall overcome it . . . The comfort is that every step I take sets me

Newman's.'"

3. Oberman, *Harvest of Medieval Theology*, 331.

nearer to my end. When I once come there, I shall both forget how long it now seems and please myself to look back upon the way that I have measured. It is thus in our passage to heaven. My weak nature is ready to faint under the very concept of the length and difficulty of this journey; my eye doth not more guide than discourage me. Many steps of grace and true obedience shall bring me insensibly thither; only let me move and hope and God's good leisure shall perfect my salvation.[4]

This mystical union is not a semi-Pelagian effort to gain favor with God, nor is it a rigid discipline for purgation of the flesh.[5] Recognizing the many false impressions this language has for Reformed Christians, this study has sought to recover this practice in a full embrace of orthodox faith that is both catholic, biblical, and evangelical and thoroughly world-engaging.

Highlighting the special emphasis that Hall placed on various types of meditation and the unique role occasional meditation had upon Protestant thought further argues that Hall was a hinge figure. His times were transitional, but his influence in occasional meditation and the value of using the created natural world would capture the attention of the famous scientist Sir Thomas Browne and the imagination of New England theologians. Jonathan Edwards could be both a theologian and a naturalist not by extolling a philosophy of romanticism but in intimating and reflecting the same line of thinking promoted by Joseph Hall. The three books of Scripture, nature, and conscience were readily employed by Puritans as valid arenas of God's playful interaction where his children are invited to taste, in part, the splendor of his glory. They were not opposed to natural theology and the many ways God's truth breaks forth in beauty and unity. The positive role of the renewed imagination was not so much a barrier or a threat but a canvas of beauty to see the love of God become more vivid to the soul of the one who takes time to see. This further beauty and this inward seeing is the great gift that Joseph Hall gave to the English world. Hall affirmed the role of *habitus fides* as a *loci* of redemptive grace operative in sanctification that provides a robust Protestant spirituality and ascetical theology often undervalued today in Reformed thought. This study reveals the complex nature of the

---

4. Hall, *Occasional Meditations*, 132.

5. Ozment, *Age of Reform*, 412: "The SE [Ignatius's *Spiritual Exercises*] built most perceptively on the interconnection of emotion, belief, and behavior. What justification by faith had attempted to accomplish for the anguished Protestant saint, Ignatius's disciplined exercises tried to do for the troubled Catholic saint. The routines it prescribed overcame old habits and prepared individuals for new states of mind and morality by playing directly on their basic emotions of fear and love. Particular sins, for example, were eliminated by attacking each with all five senses and the mind's power of imagination at regular daily intervals."

soul and faculties in relationship to faith working both in the affections and the mind as key to understanding how meditation facilitates a robust view of sanctification and lasting spiritual formation. Finally, we have seen that his influence moved beyond England to Europe and even to Russia. If a revival of interest emerges again from Hall's work, it would be a compelling and fresh impetus to reclaim the broken imagination evident in many parts of the Western church.

RECOVERING THE PRACTICE OF MEDITATION

The seventeenth century in England has been traditionally known for being a time of theological polemics, as when the shape of Protestantism in Britain was being contentiously decided. It has been less known as a period of theological retrieval in monastic mystical practices of contemplation and prayer. Bishop Joseph Hall is an important figure for understanding how the piety of meditation could be influenced by various medieval Catholic sources and still be distinctly Protestant. This study of Joseph Hall seeks to reveal not only continuity with Catholic tradition, but moreover will set forth the argument of how his own Protestant approach differed with Counter-Reformation methods in ways that affirmed the practice of meditation as both deeply English and orthodox in doctrine. There are important reasons for this clarification of approaches in meditation.

The fact that meditation needs to be rediscovered and reclaimed testifies to the various assumptions[6] about a spirituality that is both fully orthodox and firmly rooted in a faithful Christian tradition. Meditation and contemplation have a long history in ascetical theology, which can be defined in different ways as either mysticism or *sapientia*; that is, an experiential knowledge of God. Protestants can rightly claim this understanding of spirituality and also understand its history and various theological formulations. There is a need to recover the pivotal and foundational role that Bishop Joseph Hall had in the spiritual practice that was highly valued among Puritans. Furthermore, Hall is an important writer to study, not only for his influence on contemplative and ascetical theology but on the trajectory of a positive view of the imagination in the Reformed tradition. This constructive understanding in using the imagination in a redemptive function of the soul exhibited an enriched and broad spectrum of the affective theology and an affirmation of the natural world under the guidance of

---

6. For example, Hugh E. M. Stutfield claimed, "the saner Protestant does not think it is necessary in order to be pious to remain in a state of perpetual transports" (Medwick, *Teresa of Avila*, xv).

divine illumination. The historical continuity of this practice was valued by Puritans such as Thomas Watson, who asserted, "Meditation is highly commended by Augustine, Chrysostom, and Cyprian as the nursery of piety."[7] The practice of meditation was considered a type of formative matrix for the nurturing of the soul towards a love of divine realities. And the Puritans would be good guides to its cultivation. Drawing from patristic and medieval spirituality, they provided both a biblical and philosophical framework for personal sanctification in post-Reformation England. They adopted the terminology that described growing in the inward movement of the soul, without the incorporation of Neoplatonic convergence of essences, as a "wondering in the sea of Divinity."[8] For the Puritans, the language of ascent was not the terminology of esoteric introspection but the call of Scriptural holiness. "Meditation is the golden ladder by which [the saints] ascend to paradise."[9] Joseph Milosh finds the use of a ladder or scale first in the writings of Dionysius the Areopogate, and then Augustine, Jean Gerson, Walter Hilton, Richard Rolle, and in *The Cloud of Unknowing*.[10] Milosh is quoting Ruysbroek, a fourteenth-century Flemish mystic, who was an influential writer for the inspiration of the *devotio moderna* movement that was such a key source for Puritan spirituality. Hence, not everything written by Ruysbroek was commendable to later orthodoxy, but it did not negate various lines of positive influence. Furthermore, the language of these mystics is often more metaphorical, seeking to evoke the feelings of the experience. Propositional theology (one favored by Evangelicals) was not always the priority for these writers. It is also important for the validity of Protestant spirituality that true piety would have been grounded in the Bible. This was a clear distinctive tenet that separates its approach, arguably, from the esoteric mystics which tethered inward contemplation to biblical truth.

A leading scholar on spirituality, Bernard McGinn, points to 2 Corinthians 3:18 as the basis of biblical Christian mysticism—"But we all, with open face beholding as in a glass the glory of the Lord, are changed into the same image from glory to glory, *even* as by the Spirit of the Lord" (emphasis added).[11] The word translated "beholding" is referring to contemplation or the practicing of the spiritual disciplines that move a soul towards a greater experience of God's presence. Given this, it is worth considering whether

---

7. Watson, *Christian on the Mount*, 92.
8. Milosh, *Scale of Perfection*, 45.
9. Watson, *Christian on the Mount*, 92.
10. Milosh, *Scale of Perfection*, 37.
11. In this passage the apostle Paul is not speaking in a future perfect sense of our glorification in heaven, but of an ongoing, present, active tense that signifies a transformation that is happening in our earthly lives.

Reformed spirituality can be described as having a mystical side. James Packer, who loved the Puritans, with some discernment suggested the term for this is "Reformed monasticism."[12] In addition to the biblical undergirding of this piety Protestant orthodoxy would have placed a premium on the theology of divine grace without the mixture of human merit. This study affirms there is strong historical precedent to embrace the presence of mysticism in Puritan thought if rooted in a clear distinction of the relationship of grace and the transcendent nature of God's essential "otherness."[13] Neoplatonic themes that blur the lines of ontological creatureliness and Creator would be unacceptable to the biblical orthodoxy of thinkers like Herman Bavinck, critical of a mystical tradition.[14] Bavinck is right insofar as this is a generalization, but it would be wrong, in the view of this study, to place all these writers in the same category. There were various threads of mystical thought and orthodoxy that flowed from France to Germany and back to England, rich in biblical content and spirit.

Central to this thesis is this argument: there is a line of Augustinian, Benedictine, and Bernardian spirituality that viewed mystical experience as the vital outworking of experiential sanctification and growth in Christian grace, which some have called Reformed mysticism. Hence, when the Puritans incorporated the terminology of "climbing the ladder" of ascent (a common analogy of the mystical tradition), they consciously adopted a metaphor employed by previous patristic, Catholic, and Orthodox authors. Seventeenth-century English divine Bishop Joseph Hall (1574–1656) likewise used ascent language, describing sanctification as an inward pilgrimage of the soul on a ladder or mountain. More importantly, he also utilized meditative practices that run back to medieval monastic piety and patristic theology. Hall was not an innovator of a new synthesis but a faithful transmitter of his own Augustinian tradition. Henry Chadwick in his study of the prolific Bishop of Milan notes, "In a number of texts Augustine constructs a ladder of ascent with seven stages of the soul's progress in maturity of comprehension."[15] Augustine was part of a large company of orthodox

---

12. Packer, *Quest for Godliness*, 28.

13. Chan, *Spiritual Theology*, 83. Chan states, "Without this concept [grace] the Christian saint cannot be distinguished from the Buddhist ascetic with his finely contoured physique or the Confucian gentleman."

14. Bavinck, *Reformed Dogmatics*, 1:467. This is an important distinction, which Bavinck makes: "Mysticism which flourished during the Middle Ages in France and Germany sought by means of ascesis, meditation, and contemplation to attain a communion with God that could dispense with Scripture. Indeed, Scripture was needed as a ladder to ascend to this high level but became superfluous when union with God, or the vision of God, had been reached."

15. Chadwick, *Augustine: Past Masters*, 52. He cites three sources in Augustine's

spiritual writers who wrote about this ascent of the soul. Hall without qualification stood in this line as a key figure in the early seventeenth century who would influence later writers which are better known to readers today. For example, widely read works by Richard Baxter, Thomas Watson, and Jonathan Edwards were shaped and influenced by Bishop Joseph Hall. For one example, Richard Baxter wrote this concerning the worth of Hall's treatise on meditation:

> Be acquainted with this heavenly work, and thou wilt in some degree be acquainted with God; thy joys will be spiritual, prevalent, and lasting, according to the nature of the blessed object; thou wilt have comfort in life and death: when thou hast neither wealth, nor health, nor the pleasure of this world, yet wilt thou have comfort . . . Thou wilt be as one that stands on top of an exceeding high mountain.[16]

Baxter also noted in his extremely influential book *The Saint's Everlasting Rest* that he stood on Hall's work. Meditation would be an unquestioned and common practice among Protestants well into the eighteenth century in both the English church and in the American colonies. Reasons why it would lose its value is for another study, but in the first chapter it is set forth as a thesis that uncovering Hall's legacy needs to begin with learning about his historical context and the times in which he played a pivotal role prior to the English Civil War. Secondly, the period of the Restoration and later development of English church identity was not one readily amenable to the wisdom and centrist views of Bishop Hall, so sources closer to Hall were subject to sectarian interpretation. Chapter 2 puts Hall in this historical context and the key works written to address issues of spiritual formation. Terminology and the way we define these times is important to survey and acquire some sense of an objective picture of Hall as a major contributor of a Protestant approach to meditation. In chapter 3, his key work, *The Art of Divine Meditation*, will be studied in detail with commentary out of contemporaneous sources that would have been used by Hall. This presents a core part of the study, showing how Hall's understanding of meditation was rather nuanced and rooted out of an Augustinian and patristic tradition of spiritual ascent and the soul's union with Christ. Out of this discussion, chapter 4 provides the philosophical framework that argues Hall's use of faculty psychology and epistemology shaped his theological vision. The final two chapters reflect on Hall's contribution to a unique Protestant perspective on ascetical theology that touched upon controversial issues of

---

work: *De vera religione, De quantitate animae,* and *De doctrina christiana.*

16. Hall, *Contemplations on the Historical Passages,* xxx.

idolatry, images, and the proper function of the imagination. His legacy is demonstrated by the affirmation and incorporation of his model by several Puritan writers who followed him. It is in this discussion that Hall was positioned and valued as a key formative influencer of a positive use of the imagination, incorporating a sensory-based epistemology but also moving beyond it towards an Augustinian conception of experiential knowledge or *sapientia*. It is a view that factors the way God works in human hearts and reveals truth to the soul that affirmed the classic triad of Scripture, nature, and conscience: the three books of God. The supposition that Hall promoted this appreciation of "inward beauty" with the piety of ascent has great implications to a wider discussion of the way Puritans and their influence on devotional literature and the use of the imagination in other spheres such as art, science, and literature is made tenable.

Chapter 1

Recovering the Practice of Meditation

A CENTRAL FOCUS OF this book is in the meditative and ascetical theology of an English divine who was a Calvinist in theology and a Royalist Episcopalian whose moderate sentiments in a time of conflict arguably positioned him as a significant thinker. Both for his sources (Bernard of Clairvaux, St. Bonaventure, Jean Gerson, and Thomas a Kempis) and the influence he had on post-Reformation English devotional literature, Hall provides students and scholars a critical portrait for historical analysis and study. For the general reader, his insights into meditation and contemplation will be helpful for the care of the soul. Furthermore, the major role that Hall had in his *Art of Divine Meditation* on late-seventeenth-century Protestant spirituality went beyond the practice of meditation, setting forth a positive claim on the role of the imagination in theological anthropology well into the modern period. Hence, the complexity of the human soul and the interactions of its faculties in the use of meditation will be considered within a historical trajectory of theological discussions. Within this context, the epistemological questions related to medieval understandings of faith and the inter-relationship of divine revelation is important to identify. Hall affirmed the role of *habitus fides* as a *locus* of redemptive grace operative in sanctification that provided a robust Protestant spirituality and ascetical theology. Theologian Simon Chan may be right to suggest, "The Reformed tradition never developed an ascetical theology anything like 'the technique of believing God,' with the exception of certain Puritans."[1] This is a general

---

1. Chan, *Spiritual Theology*, 83.

but accurate assertion, and these certain Puritans applied meditation to their spiritual practices with clear commitment to Reformed orthodoxy as they drew from a broad range of thinking from the early church and medieval theology. Hall is also included in Chan's list of those who followed this stream of practice. We are indebted to Chan's research and his focus on ascetical theology growing from the Puritan movement. Chan comes from a Pentecostal background, but his appreciation for the Reformed tradition is very evident. Perhaps the concept of a technique would be a point of debatable interpretation. What is more certain is the contemporary need to recover this ascetical tradition that the Puritans rightly maintained as rooted in a genuine biblical understanding of nurturing the soul in greater communion with God.

English Protestants of the seventeenth century were generally astute at mining the gold of medieval monastic spirituality while at the same time denouncing "popish inventions" and other aspects of ecclesiastical oversteps. Being one of the earliest manuals on meditation written distinctively from a Reformed perspective, Hall's *The Art of Divine Meditation* (1606) was a seminal work for English spirituality. His work reflects a continuity with medieval traditions of meditative practices. This tradition and appropriation of a long history of practical piety from the medieval church highlights an interpretation that positively affirms a continuity of pre-Tridentine spirituality even as it occurs in the historical context of discontinuity with the Jesuit practices of Counter-Reformation piety.

The problem of sources will be addressed in chapter 4, but here it is enough to state that while Hall did not name all his sources, we can attest to a wide range of material both Western and Eastern that provided a rich background of a spirituality of ascent for meditation and contemplative prayer. These strains of historical material were not unknown in the seventeenth century, but the political climate created a perhaps needed sense of discretion and wisdom in how sources were cited or made public. *The Art of Divine Meditation* again was not a work in academic research for Hall, but a practical aid for every person on English soil. Hall emerged out of a complex period not easily defined, but it is necessary to follow the history and development of ways scholars have sought to define his times and the movements within them.

DEFINING BISHOP HALL

The use of terminology in historical context is vitally important for this period of study. The elusive nature of defining the term "Puritan" is, to a point, more achievable than the term "Anglican," for both are laden with modern assessments and assumptions. Bishop Joseph Hall may be classified with wearing both labels, but only with the historical qualification that the later term is anachronistic and the former more descriptive of a rather brief period of early modern English history, given the continual pressure to identify Puritanism with separatists. Christopher Hill takes a similar view of Puritans in his Marxist analysis of this period, noting that "These men, who became known as 'Puritans,' wished to see the power of bishops abolished or restricted. The clerical wing of the reformers hoped to see a Presbyterian system established."[2] W. B. Patterson asserts a modified view: "The clergy and laity of the Church of England who were the products of this tradition were not all or predominately Puritans, in the sense of wanting to alter the liturgical forms or the ecclesiastical polity of the established church in any fundamental way. Certainly, the British representatives at Dordt were not Puritans in this sense."[3] If it is sufficient to include a broad stream of Calvinistic inclined theology that is aimed at piety, as Patterson argues, then Hall would fit this readily.

Consider the complexity of this odd but accurate description of Hall: "Dordracenist deputy, Calvinist ecumenist, Erastian bishop, Joseph Hall remains a puzzle to our age as to his own."[4] Daniel Steere classifies Hall as a "moderate conforming Calvinist,"[5] and "a Calvinist Episcopalian."[6] For this study it is appropriate to refer to Bishop Hall as a Calvinistic Royalist, serving three kings and never wavering in his Reformed convictions, committed to the renewal of devotion to Christ.

Specifically, in the post-Elizabethan period up to the early part of the seventeenth century, churchmen of Reformed piety embraced both a Calvinistic orthodoxy and prelacy of the episcopate in church government.[7] As a leading delegate to the Synod of Dordt (1618–19) who referred to himself

---

2. Hill, *God's Englishman*, 22.

3. Patterson, *King James VI and I*, 279. This is a debatable point, but for the sake of following this way of nuancing the historical sense of the term "Puritanism" in this transitional age it is useful to make this distinction primarily in liturgics and ecclesiology. In terms of theology, Hall and many like him who were Conformist in their view of the established church were committed to Reformed and especially Calvinistic orthodoxy.

4. Dewar, "Bishop Joseph Hall," 5.

5. Steere, "Quo Vadis?," 15.

6. Steere, "For the Peace of Both,'" 749.

7. Collinson, *Religion of Protestants*. Collinson holds the view that this period, which Hall was a part of, allowed people with Calvinist doctrine and Royalist beliefs to coexist rather well, but later Puritans found it increasingly untenable.

as a "friendly advisor,"[8] Hall's voice was cut short when illness forced his return home, but was nevertheless very influential on its proceedings. When invited to preach before the assembly, Hall cautioned the delegates to "be not above the Scriptures, nor above the Fathers."[9] Pederson recounts Hall's centrist voice as one "who tried to mediate between those of his countrymen who accepted the synod and those who opposed it, was offered the bishopric of Gloucester, but modestly declined."[10] Hall would later become Bishop of Exeter under Charles I and then finally be given the bishopric of Norwich (1641), as Northern England was where most of the Church of England's clergy with Puritan sympathies were located.

English Royalists with Reformed sentiments like John Davenant, James Ussher, and Hall remained diligent in their theological convictions. And the Continental Reformers and divines at the Synod of Dordt held doctrinal views that were very similar to the 42 Articles of Religion. To their way of thinking, Calvinism was not an extremity but mainstream and the essence of a vital and catholic faith reformed by Scripture. When King James I sent delegates to the international Synod in Dordt, it was on the basis of a shared theological *confessionis*, not as curious onlookers. While the Synod was never officially received or endorsed in England,[11] this was not because it was considered *contra* doctrine, but supportive and instructional in explaining what the Articles affirm. This was clearly the official viewpoint ratified by the Lambeth Articles in 1595:

1. God from eternity has predestined some men to life, and reprobated some to death.
2. The moving or efficient cause of predestination to life is not the foreseeing of faith, or of perseverance, or of good works, or of anything innate in the person of the predestined, but only the will of the good pleasure of God.
3. There is a determined and certain number of predestined which cannot be increased or diminished.
4. Those not predestined to salvation are inevitably condemned on account of their sins.
5. A true, lively, and justifying faith and the sanctifying Spirit of God is not lost nor does it pass away either totally or finally in the elect.

---

8. Pederson, *Unity in Diversity*, 473.
9. Hall, *Peace among Protestants*, 485–87.
10. Pederson, *Unity in Diversity*, 281.
11. Ford, *James Ussher*, 208.

6. The truly faithful man—that is, one endowed with justifying faith—is sure by full assurance of faith (*plerophoria fidei*) of the remission of sins and his eternal salvation through Christ.

7. Saving grace is not granted, is not made common, is not ceded to all men, by which they might be saved if they wish.

8. No one can come to Christ unless it be granted to him, and unless the Father draws him: and all men are not drawn by the Father to come to the Son.

9. It is not in the will or power of each and every man to be saved.[12]

This "Genevan" view of the Reformation was the view of several influential English churchmen, such as Bishop James Ussher of Ulster, Bishop Joseph Hall of Exeter, Bishop John Davenant of Salisbury, and others, except those already convinced of an anti-Calvinist interpretation.[13] This terminology is often used pejoratively as a stricter form of Reformation theology, but Geneva itself was seen in its day as an island of fresh renewal in the progress of bringing a broad expression of Protestantism in Europe as seen in Calvin's international correspondence with those in Strasbourg, Hungary, France, and England. Nevertheless, during the move towards civil war, these men "occupied the shrinking but important middle ground between English [anti-Calvinists] on the one hand and, on the other, hardline Calvinism."[14] This Arminianism, however, was of a different breed than the one in the Netherlands.[15] The term "Arminian" on English soil tended to be oriented towards a latitudinarian view of doctrine and inclined to a robustly liturgical rubric that emphasized what Peter Lake has termed "the beauty of holiness" movement.[16] Peter Lake made an important study that shows the wide spectrum of thinking within the movement of Puritanism. In addition to liturgical concerns, the term referred more to the Royalist principle of the role of the crown in ecclesiastical matters; "the name Arminius soon became associated with the idea of the supremacy of the state over the

---

12. Bray, *Documents of the English Reformation*.

13. MacCulloch, *All Things Made New*, 318.

14. Ford, *James Ussher*, 208. Ford uses the term "Arminians" to describe these anti-Calvinists, but, as described in this study, the term can be misleading.

15. Dewar, "Ecumenical Calvinist," 5. "He suffered latterly from the unreasonableness of party hacks who labelled all loyal churchmen with the opprobrious name, 'Arminian', which had little or no connection with its Dutch origins."

16. Lake, "Laudian Style," 161.

church... the term 'Arminianism' became, surprisingly, connected with the specific position of the established Church of England."[17]

Under James I, Joseph Hall championed a middle way not between Roman Catholicism and Protestantism but between Presbyterianism and Laudianism; for Cranmer had left an indelible character and spirit of Protestantism upon England.[18] Hall's middle ground was a proverbial tightrope between radical separatism under the banner of Cromwell and his poet-Laureate John Milton and the anti-Calvinist-bent Royalists under Charles I: notwithstanding his ecclesiastical bulldog from Canterbury, the Archbishop William Laud. As J. L. Price describes the issue behind the theology: "Although the theological disputes between the Remonstrant and the Contra-remonstrants had focused on the issue of predestination, perhaps the most important issues concerned the nature of the church."[19]

Indeed, church divisions are the most insidious. Suspicious of being too much of a Puritan, Hall was "pressed" by Laud into writing a defense of episcopacy as a divine appointment, a treatise that would not reflect his irenic spirit. Despite this one exception, Hall was a moderate on matters of disputed issues. Between these two formidable foes, the Puritans and the Royalists, stood the careful balance of Joseph Hall in consistent calls for charity, peace, and moderation. This spirit is clearly seen in one of the opening sermons at the Synod of Dordt on November 29, 1618:

> We are brethren, let us also be colleagues. What have we to do with the disgraceful titles of Remonstrants, Contra-Remonstrants, Calvinists, or Arminians? We are Christians, let us also be like-minded. We are one body, let us be also of one spirit... by the most holy bowels of our Saviour Jesus Christ, seek peace, brethren, enter into peace: and so compose yourselves, that, setting aside all prejudice, and party feeling, and bad passion, we may all happily be joined in promoting the same peace... Which may He bring to pass, who is the Author of peace, the God of truth, the King of Glory; to whom, the triune God, Father, Son, and Holy Ghost, be all praise, honour, and glory, for ever and ever. Amen.[20]

Hall's desire that controlled tongues and pens would prevail in the proceedings came in the context of political tensions already present in this part of Europe as Dutch loyal to William of Orange were concerned about

17. Leeuwen et al., *Arminius, Arminianism, and Europe*, xx.
18. McCulloch, *All Things Made New*, 296.
19. Price, *Dutch Culture in the Golden Age*, 190.
20. Hall, *Peace among Protestants*, 485–87.

maintaining control in the universities and the pulpits. Hall saw, perhaps presciently, that the peace of the state would lie in the one and only King of Glory, or at least the relationship of doctrine and the social fabric of the day. Later, when Hall was back in England voicing the same sort of moderate tone, he conveyed the need for a vision of national unity that accorded with the current of Protestant orthodox doctrine. The debatable use of the term "Puritan" as applied to Hall is seen in Patterson's description, but the assertion of this Reformed light and his influence is important:

> When the moderate Puritan and future bishop Joseph Hall preached the keynote sermon to the clergy of the Convocation of Canterbury in 1624, he placed Richard Hooker in a succession of twenty-one leading scholarly lights of the Church since the Reformation; together they made the learning of the English clergy "stupor mundi," the wonder of the world. The list began with Jewel, and thereafter it was weighted towards Reformed heroes, so that Hooker was to be found cheek by jowl with the great Puritan bestseller William Perkins.[21]

To suggest that Reformed-minded ministers who remained within the Church of England, were theological anomalies, out of step with the church's *via media*, is to obscure the catholicity of the Puritan movement, and diminish the nuances of the conflicts of that period. Hall need not be cataloged among the bizarre and the unaccounted-for accident of history. Yet, he did indeed, bridge two worlds: worlds that would be moving towards a climactic clash of violence.

When the English Civil War began to loom, with the dissolution and reconvening of Parliament by Charles I for financial support (reigned 1629–40), to change metaphors, the middle ground would become a dead zone between two fronts in a theological trench warfare. As a patron of the loss cause, Hall is often forgotten not only for his efforts to stem the tide of civil war but for his major contribution in shaping English Protestant piety through his *Art of Divine Meditation*. Writing a brief biography of Hall, James Hamilton describes a breadth of scholarship which produced his work:

> The art of heavenly meditation was that which he had chiefly studied. Even among his contemporaries, there were few who combined such density of expression with such amplitude of thought—few who had studied the Fathers so diligently, and who could command them so readily—few who had drunk so deeply the classic inspiration—few who had entered into the

---

21. Patterson, *King James VI and I*, 296.

meaning of Scripture, with the same spirit of quick apprehension and thorough appreciation—and fewer still who had learned to dwell so much on high. The spirit that taught the prophets to speak, taught him to understand. In his company we feel that we are not attended by a perfunctory and hireling guide...[22]

The middle of the seventeenth century was period of intense social conflict replete with *ad hominem* polemics (John Milton being one of the most famous); biographers of Hall point to his rhetorical skills of debate from his Cambridge days, his talent for satire, and his proclivity towards debate in his first European trip among Jesuits. Some accounts reflect a new approach or change in his writing. It is not certain what the main catalyst in this shift in orientation was. Hall came upon his ordination orders, his duties in the rectory, and the favor of James I with a new and lifelong effort for conciliation and for a positive contribution towards practical and personal piety for his English church. It is highly plausible that Hall was struck with the great need to see his own people shaped more by spiritual devotion than by polemics, given his travels to Europe. He remained convinced that the theology of the Jesuits was wrong, but their devotion to piety was not to be ignored. Historian John Spurr notes, "Another Elizabethan divine, William Perkins, complained in many places of our land there is by God's blessings much teaching, yet there is little reformation in the lives of most."[23] It is this spiritual dimension of practical piety that writers from Catholic and Protestant traditions sought to address and provide a remedy. So far as placing Joseph Hall squarely in the foundation of Reformed orthodoxy, it has been thoroughly established that he belonged to the Reformed tradition found in the English Church, one he defended without qualification. His place as leading advocate for practical piety that grew out of the Puritan movement requires further understanding of the spiritual climate of the times in England, one challenged by the Counter-Reformation of Roman Catholicism.

In times of war, the nurturing of the soul is critical for maintaining balance and equilibrium. This may be a reason why there was a popular revival of personal and inner spiritual devotional practices in the seventeenth century drawn from earlier times. In England, the influence of Catholic writers was ongoing even when certain writers were suppressed by Protestant rulers for fear of Spanish sympathizers. Ignatius of Loyola (1491–1556), author of the *Spiritual Exercises*, was converted while recovering from severe battle injuries in a French hospital. He wrote his masterpiece from a journal as a guide for fellow loyal monks as a disciplined tool for spiritual growth.

---

22. Hall, *Contemplations on the Historical Passages*, xxix.
23. Spurr, *Post-Reformation*, 36.

On the other hand, the subject of this study, Joseph Hall, never saw war as a soldier, but he did see his house looted and his library almost burned, saved by quick purchase by a friend. It was church battles that threatened his times, although, as the Thirty Years' War revealed, these two realms of conflict often converged in devastating results.

His motivation for writing *The Art of Meditation* can be identified, with a degree of historical certitude, as a help for ordinary believers. He was enticed by what he saw by those influenced by Ignatius, when he saw the immense difference the use of meditation had on the cultivation of Catholic piety while on a visit to Belgium in 1602. The argument in favor of Hall's influence in English piety will show how his method provided not only an acceptable alternative to a speculative mystical piety, but a recovery of a theological strain of practice among both Reformed and Lutheran spirituality. It was a strain not fully emphasized in the first wave of English Puritans (William Ames, William Perkins) but became so common that many later Puritan divines wrote their own manuals on meditation or incorporated meditation as a principal part of everyday piety. It is this application of individual and practical use that is one point of departure from Ignatian spirituality. Later in this study, the philosophical grounding of these two approaches will be analyzed as two distinctive approaches and how that bears upon a trajectory of Protestant spirituality and view of the imagination more nuanced and varied than usually understood. There is common ground in both approaches and models but also points of departure. It is this point of departure where a brief overview is made for the purpose of providing context.

The *Spiritual Exercises* (*SE*) were influenced by the *devotia moderna*, much like Hall's method, but the Ignatian rule was primarily written for those in religious orders for a thirty-day retreat. The *SE* were later adapted and used in a variety of ways for lay participation, but it is doubtful if Loyola intended anything but a way to sharpen the hearts of the Society of Jesus in contemplative piety. So, while the *SE* were not bound to the confines of monastic life and rule, it was aimed at the religious. Beyond this difference in how they were targeted, the method offered by Hall provided a bridge between the rational and the imaginative that was not readily affirmed in Ignatian spirituality. As the *SE* were rooted in a sensory epistemology they also yielded greater authority to the church than to the Scriptures. Therefore, traditional teachings were trusted more than the senses. This is illustrated by the famous rule in the *SE*: "If we wish to be sure that we are right in all things, we should always be ready to accept this principle: I will believe that the white that I see is black if the hierarchical church so defines."[24] The magisterium of the church was the unquestioned source of authority; in the question of reason or sensory epistemology the referential point of truth objectification was in the imprimatur of *ex cathedra*.

This runs counter to the now-common assessment that (held by Louis Martz and U. M. Kauffman) that Roman Catholic practice employed the senses in ways that gave freedom to the imagination, in *contrast* to the assumption of a Reformed intellectualist view of faith with its inherent distrust in the imagination.[25] This will be elaborated on and detailed in the argument of chapter 5. Chapters 4 and 5 discuss the soul's faculties and the Reformed view of the imagination.

NEGLECT OF HALL IN RECENT HISTORY

It has not been until recently that Hall has been given the due respect as a primary figure and influencer in English practical piety. The last date of his published works (twelve volumes) was in 1879 (there were four editions of this multi-volume set in the nineteenth century), so most of his writings are not readily available today except in digital formats. Given that there is a growing publication of literature on the specific practical piety of the Puritans with increasing interest in their source material from medieval periods, it is time to remedy this gap.[26] Simon Chan is one who has provided a needed introduction to the ways Puritans in general appropriated the practice of meditation.[27] Tom Schwanda retrieved what he calls "the contemplative-mystical piety of the Puritans" in a detailed study of Isaac Ambrose.[28] A

---

24. Ozment, *Age of Reform*, 416.

25. Bavinck, *Essays on Religion, Science, and Society*, 200. Bavinck explains the intellectualist view of faith: "Whatever the case, medieval Scholasticism, with Thomas Aquinas as its principle representative, was predominately intellectual; the intellect was considered to be the most precious gift to humanity—higher and nobler than the will. It was the same with the newer philosophy introduced by Bacon and Descartes. Both branches set great store by the intellect, although the first attached greater value to sensory perception and induction and the second more to thought and the deductive method."

26. See Reuver, *Sweet Communion*. This is one example of recovery of the medievalism behind the Puritan movement.

27. See Chan, "Puritan Meditative Tradition, 1599–1691." This is a key study that has brought to the attention of contemporary scholars the importance of meditation/ascetical practice and theology.

28. See Schwanda, *Soul Recreation*. Schwanda studies the work of Ambrose and also points out the work of Hall, affirming the mystical approach of those who held to the orthodoxy of the Reformed church.

decade ago, most of the standard surveys and introductions to Reformed and English spirituality and especially Puritan piety would overlook Hall or fail to mention him as a major influence. C. J. Stranks in *Anglican Devotion* (1961) highlights the work of Jeremy Taylor and Thomas Traherne as key figures in shaping "the spiritual life of the Church of England," missing an entire generation of those who came after Thomas Cranmer and stayed within establishment ranks.[29] Stranks, who as an Anglican cleric was surveying from the Reformation to the Oxford Movement, is quite selective, and his neglect of Hall in his historical selections is a common malady. He was right in his assessment that seventeenth-century spirituality was indebted to a medieval tradition. "The growth of individual religion, which was so marked a feature of the later Middle Ages, was greatly stimulated by the Reformation with its increased emphasis on the responsibility of each soul before God."[30] The mainline Presbyterian author Howard Rice in his introductory *Reformed Spirituality* (1991) sought to recover the lost and rich spiritual tradition of the Reformation but failed to mention any contribution from Bishop Hall.[31]

Even with more well-known figures such as Richard Baxter and later Charles Spurgeon, who gave great credit to Hall and his work on meditation and contemplation, there has been little interest in the study of Hall in historical theology.[32] A revival of interest in Hall's contribution to devotional literature comes from a different field: early modern English literature. Beginning with the groundbreaking work of Louis Martz, Joseph Hall moved from the shadows behind the great metaphysical poets of Donne, Herbert, and Traherne as a key source and influence with equal literary prowess to his well-known critic and denouncer Milton, whose reputation as a Puritan is on less reliable grounds.

THE INFLUENCE OF HALL'S ART OF MEDITATION

This research will depend upon primary source documents from Bishop Hall, relevant medieval sources that influenced Hall, and the possible influence of the work of Counter-Reformation Roman Catholic authors

---

29. See Stranks, *Anglican Devotion*.

30. Stranks, *Anglican Devotion*, 13. The revision of this period by the omission of writers like Hall reveals a bias of the Oxford Movement to remove the emphasis Reformed theology had on the English Church. From a historical point, theological agendas leave a truncated view of these spiritual sources.

31. Rice, *Reformed Spirituality*.

32. There are some notable exceptions, such as the recent scholarship of Daniel Steere, "For the Peace of Both," 749–65, and "Quo Vadis?"

(primarily Francis de Sales and Teresa of Avila). English translations of these writers were being published in London and gaining public support across England.[33] It will also work from medieval/patristic authors and theologians (Augustine, Walter Hilton, Julian of Norwich, and the anonymous *Cloud of Unknowing*) who were often cited, either directly or indirectly by Hall in his interaction with ancient spiritual practices. This was true of other Caroline writers of the period, as one authority on George Herbert, states concerning the elder contemporary: "Bishop Joseph Hall, while theologically Calvinist, drew on late medieval spirituality among other sources for in his book on prayer, *The Art of Divine Meditation*."[34] Recent scholarship has studied Hall's writings have in large part come from the field of English literature. Secondary source material coming from these literary studies of Hall will be used for their ongoing interest in this period of seventeenth-century English spirituality. This study will engage in the schools of thought regarding Hall's influence upon later Reformed English divines as it relates to the system of meditation appropriated by Protestants, which both diverged and shared continuity with Roman Catholic practice.[35] Commonalities that emerge from both traditions indicate not only shared source material of the medieval texts but the divergent interpretations applied in the seventeenth century. As it pertains to the role of the Protestant application of this shared spirituality the question of how the application of the imagination has been historically tilted towards a minimization of its value. Ignatian spirituality has been understood as strongly supportive of the imagination, hence a model of a positive and expansive view of the human element. It is a view that needs to be challenged and re-evaluated in light of Hall's interpretation of this spiritual tradition.

The role of the imagination and its *loci* in the function of the soul demands a careful interaction with the philosophical tradition of understanding human faculties of the soul and the mind. The theological concerns among Protestants in using the imagination and the common misunderstandings it brings to the problem of sin and the bondage of human reason will be analyzed and defined. Defending a positive role of the imagination

33. De Sales, *Introduction to the Devout Life*; Teresa of Avila, *Santa Teresa*.

34. Sheldrake, *Heaven in Ordinary*, 5. "There is also some evidence for the influence in England of some post-Reformation Roman Catholic writers such as St. Francis de Sales, as well as the continued availability of pre-Reformation works such as Walter Hilton's spiritual treatise *The Ladder of Perfection* and the *Imitation of Christ* reputedly by the Dutch Augustinian monk Thomas a Kempis."

35. The continuity of medieval practice that is appropriated is done with a deep theological understanding of the Augustinian roots and the ability to discern the semi-Pelagian applications of views codified at the Council of Trent.

as employed by Hall has a rich theological tradition that reveals more continuity with medieval practices and will help restore a more balanced and nuanced view of a Reformed anthropology that is indebted to Calvin and builds upon his own appreciation of the *devotio moderna*. It was a balance that combined the inner heart with the outward objectiveness of revealed truth not as opposing realities but in concert that harmonized and fundamentally affirmed the interaction of the regenerated soul with the encounter of divine fellowship in union with Christ. Meditation in this perspective is not an austerely demanding ascent to the mountain of final beatification and union with God, but the "sweet kiss of Jesus" for his beloved that evokes willing hearts to ascend to great heights. It employs the imagination and what we have been calling the pre-cognitive (*habitus fidei*[36]) aspect of human understanding and enters in a knowledge that is both experiential and transcendent, rising above a dualism that posits an opposition of mystical experience and *veritas* of objective truth. Richard Muller defines this as "the God-given spiritual capacity of fallen human beings to have faith . . . the human being will not come to faith unless the *habitus fidei* is once again instilled." The use and practicality of using Hall's method is important not just in terms of historical theology and its restoration for academic relevance but for the needed application of a rich practice that should be embraced by Christians today. Aside from the popular treatments of meditation from Anglican authors like Peter Toon,[37] the practice of meditation has been either minimized along the lines of thinking deeply on Scripture (in a cognitive and objective sense) or cautioned against by Protestants from the vast literature of non-Christian, Eastern, and secular ideas of meditation. The use of the word "minimized" is used in the restricted sense and not in the sense that this type of meditation is in any way less significant, for it is foundational and necessary, as it lays the revelatory basis for essential knowledge of God that makes communion and contemplation a possibility. If the objective basis is removed, then the argument for a Reformed mysticism falls back into an undefinable subjective sense of experience set against rational truth. Again, another binary false choice if we follow the way of Bishop Hall.

Imaginative use of Scripture is often relegated to "Romish fantasy" or as dangerous allegorical hermeneutics with a door to the mystical essence of the unknowable. Caution flags are waved, and those committed to orthodoxy keep their distance. A study of Hall reveals that there is a third

---

36. Muller, *Dictionary of Latin and Greek Theological Terms*, 146.

37. Toon, *From Mind to Heart*. There are several attempts to introduce meditation to a Protestant readership that in my view do not rise to the level as Toon. See Toon, *Meditating as a Christian*. There is also a new work by Saxton, "God's Battle Plan for the Mind."

option that rises above the need to decide in an either/or fashion and mistakenly define meditation in a reductionistic way as merely a function of the intellect or memory on the one hand, and, on the other, view meditation as speculative mindlessness. Hall was providing his readers with a mindful meditation that engaged the heart, the intellect, and the will. Humans are more than "rational souls," whether defined either by the idealism of Plato or the rationalism of Rene Descartes (1596–1650).

Human beings are embodied souls or soulful bodies[38] who think as well as feel, who reason as well as desire, and see with eyes open and imagine with inner eyes of faith, the mystery of godliness. This concept is rooted deeply in Augustinian thought. "Man is neither the soul alone nor the body alone, but body and soul together."[39] The nineteenth-century Dutch theologian Herman Bavinck (1854–1921) stated as few can:

> We have innate capabilities, qualities, habits, dispositions, inclinations, conditions, actions, and whatever else one wants to call them, prior to our consciousness and our will, they shape us to be what we are and lay the foundation for our thinking and acting. Without our will or knowledge, all that unconscious [dimension] affects our conscious life and gives direction and guidance.[40]

The inner recesses of the soul where precognitive understanding provides the nursery or the *habitus* of faith is the realm where imagination (wordless thinking) shapes our desires and informs our understanding and enlightens our thinking. As Bavinck concludes, "Our becoming aware and our observations, our feeling, our wanting, our thinking and speaking; all our convictions in religion, morality, science, the arts; our insights and prejudices, our sympathies and aversions—these all are rooted far and deep behind the consciousness in our soul."[41] Hall is also an example of providing the kind of balance in how the knowledge of the heart is not merely a given in the processing of spiritual truth. One can know something without really having love. As Hall clearly affirmed, "for if there be some that have much zeal, little knowledge; there are more that hath much skill and no affection

---

38. Thiselton, *Thiselton Companion to Christian Theology*, 786. He states that "Aquinas denies the second-century Stoics and Tertullian that the soul is corporeal." He appeals to Augustine: the soul "is not extended quantitatively through the body."

39. Thiselton, *Thiselton Companion to Christian Theology*, 786. He is quoting Augustine. This is also the view of Calvin: "There can be no question that man consists of a body and a soul, meaning by soul, an immortal though created [contra Origen] essence, which is his nobler part" (Calvin, *Institutes* I.15.2).

40. Bavinck, *Essays on Religion, Science, and Society*, 186.

41. Bavinck, *Essays on Religion, Science, and Society*, 186.

may do good to others by information of judgment, but shall never have thanks, either of his own heart or of God, who useth not to cast away his love on those whom he is but known, not loved."[42] It is in the affections as Hall understood this vital connection between knowledge that was formed in the soul or the conscious mind and the precognitive desires and longings of the will. It was a nuanced view of the soul and its faculties built upon an Augustinian framework of epistemology that intersected with soteriological implications. While Hall may have shared insights of practical processes in the application of meditation with Ignatian and Salesian models, it did not imply similar foundations in the role of grace and justification as Protestants understood *sola de gracia* and *justi de fides*. This clear distinction is important in the ongoing discussion of how Hall appropriated a practice of mystical theology that steered clear of semi-Pelagian views of grace.

REFORMED MYSTICISM

The way these two kinds of knowing are balanced in a Reformed view of meditation is central to understanding Hall's contribution. Hall bridged the two poles of knowledge and the gap between the doctrines of Reformed orthodoxy and the practice of ascetical traditions for a contemporary English context that emerged in a modern period.

The experiential or *sapientia* knowledge[43] that was central to the late medievalist mystics of the *devotia moderna* was a concept central in highlighting the role of one's heart in apprehending the knowledge of God.[44] Protestants such as Joseph Hall (1574–1656), Richard Baxter (1615–91), and John Bunyan (1628–88) to Jonathan Edwards (1703–58) are often seen as moving from the mainstream of Reformed theology or at least overcorrecting a scholastic tendency (see for example Louis Martz).[45] This study

---

42. Hall, *Works*, 3:48.

43. *Sapientia* is distinguished from *scientia*—it is a knowledge based on sensory and rational process. Augustine states it is this intellectual and contemplative knowing that leads to love and is preferred over mere knowledge of external things. See Augustine, "On the Trinity," XIV.14, 163. Speaking about earthly knowledge, he states it "differs from contemplation of eternal things; and the latter is reckoned to wisdom, the former to knowledge . . . the knowledge of the contemplation of God, which will be the highest reward of the saints."

44. Beeke, "Calvin on Piety," 125. This priority of the heart over head in the experiential piety of Calvin is argued by Beeke as a major theme in understanding Calvin and the Puritans. This should be seen as a priority that puts an emphatic role of the heart in the relationship of the soul and not an exclusion of the mind. It is a guard against both rationalism and subjectivism in a theory of knowledge.

45. Martz, *Poetry of Meditation*.

will seek to correct that perception and reveal more continuity with both Calvin and the pre-Reformed tradition of the *devotia moderna*. The justification of seeing the universal and catholic contribution of Reformed writers as part of the ongoing reformation of Christ's church is needed today to foster better appreciation for a distinctive Protestant appropriation of spiritual practices to shape the heart and soul towards an experiential knowledge of God. In our times, the growing popularity of non-Christian forms of meditation and the misunderstanding that views Puritan polemics and theology as a new scholasticism which were mainly concerned with the role of reason to the exclusion of the affective and volitional aspect of the human soul presents a critical need to give Joseph Hall a new appraisal. As previously noted, Hall bridged the gap between the doctrines of Reformed orthodoxy and the practice of ascetical traditions for an English context. Beyond the historical interest of Hall's influence in the seventeenth century, there are important practical rewards for recovering his work for contemporary studies. The spiritual, sanctifying, and therapeutic benefit of his method of contemplation and its practical application is an untapped source for our age of broken imaginations.

On one side of the question there are important philosophical issues. There has been recent work on the dynamic role of the Holy Spirit in Protestant orthodox theology and the implications of an Augustinian/Thomist epistemology by Richard Muller.[46] Muller makes the case that Protestant orthodoxy coming from the Puritans could use Thomistic terms without importing the whole system of rationalism and its underpinnings of semi-Pelagian theology.

The religious imagination that formed the basis of a rich spirituality that embodied the role of the senses from the work of Bernard, Calvin, and the Puritans from the *Nadere Reformatie*[47] on the Continent and the English Puritans still needs to be studied in light of this important imaginative theology's contribution to the flourishing of literature, art, and music in subsequent Protestant spirituality. There is still an imbalanced view of how the Puritans valued the imagination and provided positive direction both for a theology of aesthetics[48] and for practical piety. Bishop Hall, in large part, paved the way for this imaginative theology to grow and develop in a uniquely Calvinistic framework. Even within the history of iconoclastic

---

46. Muller, *After Calvin*, 99–100.

47. Reuver, *Sweet Communion*. Note the relation of the Dutch Further Reformation to English piety.

48. Aesthetics and the role of the arts, literature, and culture in relationship to theology is seen as secondary, but it reveals the historical development and influence of Puritan thinking outside the bounds of the ecclesiastical structures.

wars and polemical theology, the role of the imagination was not diminished but further refined and utilized in ways that affirmed God's creation, natural revelation, and the human soul as the *loci* of a dynamic spiritual encounter with God, yet still within a classic paradigm of creaturely fallenness and human inability apart from redemptive grace.

The debate in recent years over Hall's use and appropriation of an epistemology that diminished the faculty of the imagination was limited in literary circles.[49] This discussion will compare the role of meditation presented by Ignatius of Loyola (1491–1556) and his use of the senses and its interplay in the imagination in noncognitive experience and the way Hall restricted the imagination in a minimalistic manner. This writer will argue against that thesis and posit a view that understands that there are many similarities between the two methods. Hall's understanding of the imagination and line of influence, while in a way minimalistic, encouraged a more pronounced role of the imagination than the realism of a restrictive sensory-based epistemology. The fact that Hall could meditate on a bee or a river gives credence to this. Belden Lane, in his own way, challenges the prevailing academic prejudice in asserting, "The Puritan grasp of Christian truth was one which above all laid hold of the majestic and untamed God of Calvinism. Of course, in doing so it risked being utterly overwhelmed by that which it sought to apprehend. John Calvin had opened the Puritan imagination to the vast landscapes of fear, double-edged as they are by splendor and awe."[50] Taking the examples of Hall's application of meditation in his other works and his occasional meditations, the role of the imagination, while not unbridled, is re-imagined by divine grace for holy contemplation. Beyond the role of personal piety, there are indicators, indeed evidence, that this provided a rich cultural imagination that shaped the modern period. If one can argue the Renaissance movement that influenced art, music, and literature in seventeenth-century England flourished outside the rigid confines of religious and ecclesiastical *imprimatur* to explore the natural beauty of the common and the secular, then English Puritanism, in some forms, promoted a theological minimalism that cautioned the restrictions of a realism that encroached upon transcendency rather than guarded its awe and other

49. Martz, *Poetry of Meditation*. A debate that is found in literary studies, but it has deep implications in theological issues (Huntley, *Bishop Joseph Hall*). In this thesis, it is argued that Huntley takes a more nuanced view than Martz and Kaufmann, who see Hall as restrictive in his use of the imagination. Huntley presents a strong case with extensive study of Hall's work and sources.

50. Lane, *Landscapes of the Sacred*, 105. See also Lane, *Ravished by Beauty*. Written by a Reformed thinker who teaches at a Jesuit university, Lane often puts an emphasis on commonalties of spirituality and its retrieval of a positive theology of beauty. The historical theology of these traditions is not his primary concern.

worldliness. Shakespearian drama, the music of lutist John Dowland, the art and emblems (wood engravings) exploding in the print industry, and the imaginative poetry of the Caroline poets[51] argue in favor of this minimalist and even Calvinistic bent; not condemnations against the imagination, but against a fallen and materially restricted one.

---

51. Sheldrake, *Heaven in Ordinary*, 4–6.

Chapter 2

A Puritan Primer in Reformed Devotion

Is a Puritan ascetical theology merely running on the coattails of Catholic spirituality? It is a question that assumes a modern assessment that Tridentine spirituality was the essential and sole inheritor of medieval piety. As the first chapter argued, the continuity in the Protestant expression of this spirituality is found in authors such as Joseph Hall. It is especially true in the case for reassessing Puritan piety as belonging to this tradition and not an intellectualist rejection or restriction of the imagination. This chapter discusses that direct line of continuity. Being one of the earliest Protestant manuals on meditation, Bishop Hall's *The Art of Meditation* laid the groundwork for further refinement by later Puritan authors. This tradition and appropriation of a long history of the *practical piety* from the medieval church highlights an interpretation that positively affirmed a continuity of catholic pre-Tridentine spirituality even as it occured in the historical context of discontinuity with the Jesuit practices of Continental post-Reformation and Counter-Reformation piety. Joseph Hall once referred to the system of the Jesuits as "crabbed theology."[1] Ignatian methodology and rules were too confining with rigor and discipline than the options favored by Hall.

The question is how directly Bishop Hall drew from Ignatius of Loyola's *Spiritual Exercises* or whether his appropriation of a "method" signals a new direction for a Reformed *piety* or a corrective return to a more Augustinian and Bernardian ascetical theology. The first option would be more of an adaptation for contextual reasons, the second would be more of

---

1. Hall, *Works*, 11:473.

a retrieval of something already in its own tradition. In one view, Hall may be considered as merely plagiarizing a Roman Catholic spiritual practice to augment a spiritually deficient but heavily doctrinal orientation of English Puritanism. Another view can argue the presence of an ongoing trajectory of spiritual practices that was both catholic and trans-Continental in origin and influence. This latter view will be the argument developed in this work; that is, Hall was retrieving within his own spiritual tradition sources that were both catholic and orthodox.

HALL'S LIFE AND WORK: EXEMPLAR OF RELATIONAL ORTHODOXY

Joseph Hall (1574–1656) lived in a time of great ecclesiastical and political shifts. While he was a committed Calvinist in theology, he was not a separatist or militant Conformist in his ecclesiology.[2] Reformed in convictions, he was catholic in spirit.

He was appointed dean of Worcester by King James I (serving 1603–25) and made bishop of Exeter under King Charles I (1627) but was expelled from office under Cromwell and briefly imprisoned in the infamous Tower of London. He died in 1656, holding the title of Bishop of Norwich, having watched the desecration of Norwich's cathedral and the destruction of his personal library thirteen years earlier by Cromwellian soldiers (1643). Garnering the suspicions of both Puritans and Laud, Hall remained an enigma of moderation in a day of intractable polarizations. At the Synod of Dordt (1618–19), Hall was distinguished as a moderate voice among political and theological factions. There was a call to charity and mutual respect in his farewell sermon to the international assembly as sickness necessitated his early departure. Drawing his text from Ecclesiastes 7:15, "Be not righteous over much, neither make thyself over wise," Hall gave this appeal to the delegates. "Our age is perishing from too much knowledge . . . We all desire to know everything . . . we foolishly rush and attempt to go headlong into the most secret councils of God."[3] It was an admonishment of maintaining a humble and respectful moderate stance over disputable matters of predestination and above all to never move beyond the Scriptures and the ancient fathers.

As a scholar he is recognized as a poet, satirist, and even referred to as the "English Seneca."[4] Yet he is not typically named among the metaphysical

---

2. Huntley, *Bishop Joseph Hall*, 88.
3. Hall, *Works*, 11:479.
4. Kinloch, *Life and Works of Joseph Hall*, 88.

poets of English literature such as Herbert, Donne, and Traherne, even though he was their equal in literary output. His early work, begun while at Cambridge and finished at Hawstead, *Mundus Alter et Idem*, was a brilliant work of imaginative travel to an upside-down world, where all values and virtues were paradoxically flipped. In the mythical country he called Moronia Felix, he writes about the worship of the goddess Fortune:[5]

> On the summit of the mountain there shines a crystal palace, formed (according to the estimation of the neighbors) not by human hands; for they claim that once upon a time Fortune, driven away from heaven and from the band of the gods, erected her throne here, an equivalent of heaven. From here she assists mortals with her aid and with her gifts, and she bestows her inexhaustible wealth with so generous a hand that whatever worthy person will seek her with a trusting mind will not fail to obtain eventually whatever he desires, once he has waited long enough. From all regions of the earth, from every ages, sex, and rank of life, people flock here; however, most frequently they come from *Moronia Pia*. There is scarcely anybody in the whole world either so impotent, or so extraordinary, who has not at some time gazed upon this mountain and ascended it, when he has been allowed.[6]

Hall took aim at the false ascent (or vain contemplation) of both worldly philosophy and false religion as imaginary ascents to a fantastical paradise. Like the biblical tower of Babel, Hall used this satirical device of dystopia to wittingly disarm the dangers of his own day. Hall did not put his name on the early publications, but it was assumed he was the author by Milton, who attacked his style of writing. Subsequent scholarship has supported the thesis that the author was indeed Hall and his biographers have not questioned it. Referred to as one of the early examples of dystopian novels, the work takes aim at hypocrisies, extremities in life, and lack of moderation. It was critical of those who traveled far on pilgrimages and was sardonic of Roman Catholics in the search for holy places.[7] There are

---

5. Fortune is the goddess of fools, and Moronia Felix is the country of "happy ignorance."

6. Wands, *Another World and Yet the Same*, 97. The early edition with a preface from Hall's friend William Knight has the full title, *Another World and Yet the Same, or the Southern Continent, before this Always Unknown, Through the Extended Travels of a Wandering Academic Most Recently Surveyed, Author: Mercurius Britannicus*. The first English translation was by John Healey in 1609 and was entitled *The Discovery of a New World*; see John Miller Wands's edition, *Another World and Yet the Same*, iv.

7. Elsewhere Hall expresses the danger of travel—even though Hall traveled quite a lot for a cleric of that day. Hall, *Works*, vol. 10.

aspects of the narrative and viewpoints that were in contrast to Milton's own life and questionable reputation. It was in this sense double-edged against all forms of extremity, either to libertines or towards unquestioned conformity. Always presenting to his audience a middle course, Bishop Hall presented the errors of both ignorance and vice.[8] This work is pointed out as an example, as an indication of the type of issues that Hall was addressing, especially at empty religion. The reason for Hall departing from this kind of satire literature stemmed most likely from his vocational and spiritual concerns of shepherding his congregations and diocese. He retreated from scholarly literary polemics to the role of a pastor and churchman to champion the spiritual life and the shaping of English piety.

As a pastor, his first published work was *Meditations and Vows* (1605), a work that would reflect a lifelong interest in the inner life of piety and the valuable use of meditation for spiritual devotion. This early interest would result in his major contribution—to the devotional practice of meditation/contemplation and the piety of English Puritan spirituality. *The Art of Divine Meditation* (1606) was a seminal work that expressed a Reformed approach to meditation that, while similar in form, departed from the philosophical underpinnings of Loyola's *Spiritual Exercises* in use on the Continent. It was during a visit to the Lowlands that Hall experienced what has been a called a turning point in his thinking as he was introduced to the firsthand evidence the formative discipline of the Jesuits had on shaping the religious practice on so many people.[9] An English version of the *Spiritual Exercises* was written by Jesuit Edward Dawson in 1614, with the title *The Practical Method of Meditation*. Ironically, it bears a close resemblance to Hall's work on meditation.[10] The post-Elizabethan settlement times he lived in were deeply suspicious of anything like "aides and popish ceremonies" in part because of anti-Jesuit sentiments after the Gunpowder Plot of 1605. "The seventeenth century experienced a post-Reformation context between

---

8. Wands, *Another World and Yet the Same*, xlii.

9. Huntley, *Bishop Joseph Hall*, 18. Huntley notes, "The trip was a turning point in Hall's thinking on the Christian duty of meditation. Hall accepted the invitation, he tells us in his autobiography, 'for the great desire I had to inform myself ocularly of the state practice of the Romish church, the knowledge whereof might be of no small use to me in my holy station' . . . Hall began to think deeply about meditation, particularly for Protestants, as he became aware of the superior discipline in this genre maintained by the Jesuits he met on the Continent, a discipline stimulated by the *Spiritual Exercises* of St. Ignatius of Loyola." This study argues the point that while he was impressed with this devotion, Hall did not seek to appropriate this work for a Protestant readership. There are more reasons and influences to indicate his work was more widely rooted in source material.

10. Martz, "Meditation," 1086.

several versions of Reformation. Disagreeing with each other about the most fundamental questions such as the constitution of the true church, the economy of salvation, or the nature of meaningful worship . . . naturally laid claim to the legacy and rhetoric of the Reformation."[11] These were his times; a closer look at Hall's formative education provides another contextual lens to view him.

Hall was born on July 1, 1574, at Bristow Park to devoted Calvinistic parents. His early childhood was nurtured under the tutelage of a Puritan-leaning parish minister, Anthony Gilby. His intellectual acumen was noticed by his pastor. Hall was an excellent student and enrolled in Emmanuel College at Cambridge, a relatively new school established under Elizabeth I for training Puritan clergy. At Emmanuel, the young Hall reflected a bent towards the arts and literature evident in his writings and collegiate activities like poetry and drama. Frank Huntley states, "Pre-eminent in every part of the curriculum, Joseph Hall was also the poet of Emmanuel College."[12] By 1596, Hall received his master's degree and a year later his first work in satire was published. His secular works of satire and fiction, *Virgidemiae* (1596) and *Mundus Alter et Idem* (1605), were recognized by peers and scholars as examples of fine Renaissance literature and indicated the possible road of success as a poet he could have trod if he had not turned to a life of service in the Church of England and as a writer of devotional literature.

He was ordained in 1603, the same year King James IV of Scotland was crowned as James I of England. After an undesirable time of serving as a "house chaplain" under Sir Robert Drury at Hawstead, with meager pay so that he had to "write books to buy books,"[13] he caught the attention of James, who enlisted his support of episcopacy among the Scots at Hampton Court in 1604. The tensions being somewhat heightened from this political mandate gave leverage to conspiracy-minded papists to place explosives under the House of Parliament. As the infamous Gunpowder Plot was uncovered and its guilty conspirators tried by court, populists' sentiments were rapidly moving away from the "old religion" of Rome in a nationalistic impulse, if for any other reason (politics is often the horse driving the carriage of religious devotion). In this time, he was offered the opportunity to travel to the Continent with Lady Anne Drury's brother, Sir Edmund Bacon. According to his own account, he desired to see for himself "the state and practice of the Romish church."[14] This was a formative trip, for upon his return to

---

11. Spurr, *Post-Reformation*, 36.
12. Huntley, *Bishop Joseph Hall*, 7.
13. Wands, *Another World and Yet the Same*, xxii.
14. Hall, *Works*, 1:xxxix.

England he wrote his most influential work, *The Art of Divine Meditation*. This would not be his only trip to Europe, but it was his first exposure to the practice of spiritual disciplines of the Jesuits among devoted Roman Catholics that made a deep impression upon him. Hall was not simply a plagiarizer of Ignatius, for as Huntley states, "after the trip to the Low Countries, Hall's view of meditation is instinct not with St. Ignatius of Loyola but with a much older tradition: the Bible, the devotional spirit of *Windesheim*, the medieval naivete of the Augustinian monks, and Neoplatonism rather than Thomism."[15] He had a deep interest in the biblical books of wisdom, and wrote a contemplation engaging in the Song of Songs in Hall's *Solomon's Divine Arts* (1609).

When Hall was the preacher of Waltham Holy Cross, he gave a sermon before the court of King James I. The king must have recognized a rising theological light, and James would place him near positions of trust and as a theological advisor to the throne. There were political reasons for this as well, for Hall was both a Calvinist and a Conformist, and was loyal to the crown, providing James important mediation with the Presbyterians during the contentious Hampton Court meetings and a trusted delegate to the Synod of Dordt (1618) even though sickness required an early departure. This unexpected absence did not lessen the esteem the Synod had for him: while every British delegate received a silver medallion as a sign of appreciation, Hall's medallion was the only one in gold, which he wore proudly throughout his life, claiming to "live and die in the suffrage of that synod of Dordt."[16] The medal is now on display in the Fitzwilliam Museum at Cambridge and depicts the assembly on one side and on the other side a large mountain with two pilgrims climbing the summit against a torrent of wind with the words inscribed: *Erunt ut mons Sion*, "They shall be even as Mount Sion." After Dordt, the king offered Hall the bishopric of Gloucester, and he declined the offer, content to be dean of Worcester. It would be under Charles I that Hall was made Bishop of Exeter in 1627 and thereafter became increasingly engaged in the battles of ecclesiastical issues, ever keeping a moderate stance between schismatic Nonconformists and the ire of Laud.

Several works by Hall denounced the problems of Rome and the excesses of groups like the separatists. His letters written to the Jesuit Marco

---

15. Huntley, *Bishop Joseph Hall*, 73.

16. Huntley, *Bishop Joseph Hall*, 109. So far, this researcher had not discovered any sources that might disclose the reason for Hall being singled out for this unique and special honor. It was a gift that the bishop would have been grateful for and one he made sure was listed in his will. The good bishop may have been deposed of his charge because of his Erastian views; it was never because he departed from his Calvinistic beliefs.

Antonio De Dominis (1556–1624) are characteristic of his skills of rhetoric and polemics with the aim of restoring relationships. Marco Antonio De Dominis was a defector from Rome who wrote several works attacking the Roman Church. He was given safe refuge and a pension by King James I. Later, De Dominis recanted and sought to return to Rome. His perceived heresies were not welcomed, as the die was cast for the man. Yet, his presence in England as a Protestant convert was illustrative of the metropolitan climate of London. It is also a picture of the kind of ecumenical spirit and culture that James sought to foster in England with Catholics, Orthodox, and Protestants. It was a dream that did not materialize in his day.

> Hall, then dean of Worcester, pointed to the dangers which would confront De Dominis in the city of seven hills which the archbishop's thunderbolts had so often struck. Assuming that De Dominis was still committed to Christian unity, Hall argued that Rome had shown no signs of weakening in its opposition to those outside its ranks, nor was Rome likely to yield to entreaties to give up its claims to spiritual and temporal authority or its own distinctive doctrines. The dean seemed frankly puzzled that one whom the English Church had welcomed and the king himself had bountifully entertained would now leave his newly made friends. Did the archbishop find the religion of the English, which he had once extolled, to be lacking in divine truth? Hall reminded De Dominis of the inquisitorial prison in which certain English visitors in Rome had spent some seventeen years. The English theologian predicted that if De Dominis did not change his mind and remain in his adopted country, he would wish either that he had never seen Britain or else that he had never left it.[17]

Hall was right in his prediction, because when De Domini returned to Rome it was not with welcome arms. He was imprisoned for being a heretic and would die unreconciled either to Rome or to the Protestant faith.[18] Returning to the work of devotional interests Hall published *Occasional Meditations* (1630) and *A Plaine and Familiar Explication (by way of Paraphrase) of all the hard texts of the whole Divine Scripture of the Old and New Testament* (1633), revealing his biblical scholarship tilted toward

---

17. Patterson, *King James VI and I*, 252.
18. Patterson, *King James VI and I*, 257. Patterson notes that De Domini was received with suspicion but kept and provided for by Pope Gregory XV, and upon the pope's death De Dominis was placed in prison, where he died (1624). He was condemned as a relapsed heretic posthumously on December 21, 1624, and his body and books were burned.

the benefit of his diocese and congregants. He wrote *Christian Moderation* (1640) and later that year a small work defending episcopacy (*Episcopacie by Divine Right*) at the request of Archbishop Laud to ensure his loyalty to the Church of England. Huntley makes the case that this was the trigger for the famous Smectymnuans controversy. Puritans more intent on separatist views could no longer stand with Hall. But as Huntley notes, the villainy of rhetoric came from Milton and was responded to by a friend of Hall and not the work of Joseph Hall.

> I have argued elsewhere that it was Milton, not Hall, who began the game of "grim laughter" and who went far beyond Hall in personal abuse. And I think I have made a good case for the Reverend Robert Dunkin, an Anglican rector in Cornwall from Hall's diocese, as the author of *A Modest Confutations* (1642), the pamphlet that begot Milton's angriest prose, and not Hall himself.[19]

In November of 1641, Hall was given the Bishopric of Norwich, but before he could take his charge, he was imprisoned in the Tower for a few months just in time for a London winter with twelve other bishops.[20] During this time he wrote *The Devout Soul: Rules of Heavenly Devotion*, but it wasn't published until later by his son (1644). Upon release, he sought to discharge his newly appointed duties over his diocese, which historically was partial to those of Calvinist leanings from Emmanuel College. The diocese of Norwich came to be known as a haven for Puritan-minded priests. His residence in the bishop's house was shortlived, and his family was forced to move into a cottage and his library saved from the fires by the intervention of a wealthy lady who purchased them. These events are recorded in his tract *Hard Measure*, written in May 1647 and later published in his posthumous book, *The Shaking of the Olive-Tree*. The radical nature of this iconoclasm driven by zealous mobs was described by Hall in his own pen:

> Sheriff Toft, and Alderman Lindsey, attended with many zealous followers, came into my chapel to look for superstitious pictures and relics of idolatry, and send for me, to let me know they found those windows full of images, which were very offensive and must be demolished. I told them they were pictures of some ancient and worthy bishops, as St. Ambrose, Austin, etc. It was

---

19. Huntley, *Protestant Meditation*, 17.

20. Hall would affirm a more moderate view of the episcopate in his work *The Shaking of the Olive Tree* (1659), edited with some of his remaining works by his son. See Hall's first work, entitled *Peace of Rome* (1641), and his *Defense of the Humble Remonstrance Against the Frivolous and False Exceptions of Smectymnuans*.

answered me that they were so many popes; and one younger man amongst the rest (Townsend, as I perceived afterwards) would take upon him to defend that every diocesan bishop was a pope. I answered him with some scorn and obtained leave that I might with the least loss and defacing of the windows give order for taking off that offense, which I did by causing the heads of those pictures to be taken off, since I knew the bodies could not offend.[21]

One can picture how Hall would preserve most of these windows by his swift thinking and how in this confrontation with an angry mob, he was able to speak with a cool and balanced mind to senseless rampaging. Both beauty and truth were of equal value to him.

Hall continued to preach throughout his diocese, ordaining ministers in his home, and wrote several works of a devotional nature, moderate in tone, Calvinist in theology, and irenic in spirit. Even with little income and declining health, Hall would continue to write and publish. In 1647, he authored three books of a rich devotional nature, *Satan's Fiery Darts Quenched*; *An Holy Rapture: or Pathetical Meditations of the Love of Christ*; and *Christ Mystical*. The last of those became very popular in the nineteenth century in part due to the advocacy and influence of General Gordon, the well-known British officer who loved Hall's stress on the heart's devotion to Christ. General Gordon was a respected military leader who died in Sudan defending a British post whose reinforcements from England were delayed for a year. His edition of the book was printed in 1893, revealing an interest in Hall in the nineteenth century. Interestingly, Gordon was drawn to the mystical side of the Christian faith and never formally joined any church. A Hollywood film about Gordon highlighted his heroism and his idiosyncrasies, fashioning him like an British George Patton.

Hall was succinctly described by fellow Puritan and historian Thomas Fuller as "Bishop of Exeter, then Bishop of Norwich, then Bishop of no place, surviving to see his sacred function buried before his eyes."[22] Bishop Hall died on September 8, 1656, with no wealth, no cathedral, but the legacy of a godly ministry in declaring the truths of a gospel-enriched Calvinism to a nation tossed in a flurry of ecclesiastical battles. Hence, we might dub him as the patron of lost and hopeless causes in a time of civil and religious divisions.

This historical context is important considering the growing popularity of Ignatian and Salesian spiritual practices in Roman Catholic countries amid the Counter-Reformation work of Jesuit missionaries. While he

21. Dupré and Saliers, *Christian Spirituality*, 68.
22. Fuller, *History of the Worthies of England*, 130.

debated with Jesuits and corresponded with a Jesuit convert, De Domini, who, as previously noted, was returning to Rome again, Hall revealed a sensitivity to common sources and a commitment to Reformed convictions. Patterson states how Hall and De Domini corresponded with each other:

"The *Second Manifesto* seems to have been written as a kind of spiritual purgation of one determined to show that he was free from heresy. Most revealing is a long letter written while De Dominis was still in England in response to a letter from the theologian Joseph Hall, who had written to try to dissuade the archbishop from his plan to return to Rome."[23] There is a deep respectful tone in this correspondence, and it reveals how Hall used theological sources in a way to convey to his friend the biblical and apostolic theology of the Church of England and of Protestants in general. To coin a term, Hall was a premiere exponent of "relational orthodoxy."

In addition to the polemical side of these arguments, there was the spiritual impact of Catholic writers from Spain. Teresa of Avila's *Vida* was published in London in 1623, and its popularity was noted in the poetry of Richard Crashaw.[24] Crashaw's poems on Teresa were very popular in England and point to the wide readership of this Spanish mystic among both Protestants and Roman Catholics. A woman devoted to prayer and contemplation was in similar company to Julian of Norwich and the English tradition of holy women or "gentlewomen." It is noteworthy for context that Saint Teresa was not favored by the Jesuits and was herself under trial by the Inquisition. Mystics were often an unlucky lot that got caught in the crossfires of politics and strongly drawn boundaries.

INFLUENCES AND SOURCES: DEVOTIO MODERNA

In content and methodology, Hall's style and philosophical framework reinforced a view of human psychology closely identified with Augustinian/Thomistic anthropology. Secondly, he acknowledged his debt to the ascetical theology of Jean Gerson, the University of Paris chancellor and arguably the leader of the *devotio moderna*, a movement beginning in the Netherlands by the Brethren of the Common Life, exemplified by Thomas a Kempis's influential work *The Imitation of Christ*. The *devotio moderna* and Augustinian epistemology paved the way for imaginative use of the sensory-based knowledge and pre-cognitive innate proclivities to engage the whole soul in reflecting on creation, our redemption in Christ, and the inner thoughts of the heart—the three *loci* of ascetical theology, or the three books of knowing

---

23. Patterson, *King James VI and I*, 252.
24. Medwick, *Teresa of Avila*, 251. See Rapley, *Lord Is Their Portion*, 47.

God: Scripture, nature, and conscience.[25] Chrysostom was one who identified the first two books of God: the Book of the Creatures and the Book of the Scriptures. The first book prepares the hearers to be able to hear the second book, but the relationship between the two is complementary, not in opposition. Conscience was understood later as a *locus* of the Spirit's work as well by Augustine, Aquinas, and, later, the Puritans. Out of this understanding Hall wrote his *Art of Divine of Meditation*. It reflected a long historical development of medieval practice and Augustinian theology. Its unique contribution as a Protestant ascetic practice represented more than appropriation of Catholic sources but a retrieval of spirituality from early patristic and medieval theology consistently received by many Protestant writers. This chapter provides the context to read his text and to understand how his method provided individual believers not a tight rule but a roadmap for a soul's journey in love of God. Chapter 3 presents the case through commentary that Hall retrieved a tradition that English Protestants could claim as their own and as true to the catholicity of their faith.

---

25. See Lane, *Landscapes of the Sacred*, 104.

Chapter 3

The Art of Meditation: Analysis

THE MEDITATION THAT WAS promoted by Hall was Protestant in application, but it was indebted to monastic practice and history. It is a central thesis of this study that ascetical theology rooted in patristic and Augustinian thought was not a foreign invasion into the piety of the seventeenth-century Puritan practice of contemplative prayer. Neither was it a result of Neoplatonic views influencing post-Reformation orthodoxy. Hall's contribution to meditation was a retrieval of biblical and early church spirituality, at points contextualized, but always faithfully transmitting the ancient tradition of contemplation and the way of holiness. This was reflected in this commentary on the *Art of Divine Meditation*, where, along with citations from Hall, notations and parallels will be drawn from a broad range of patristic and medieval voices. One Lutheran scholar put it succinctly, "The heart of Puritan, as of monastic devotion, was prayer and meditation."[1] In application, Hall's *Art* was reaching beyond the concerns of monastic, and therefore specialized, hierarchical spirituality towards a practice available for every believer, flexible in usage and concerned with pedestrian realities. This was seen in the original full title, *The arte of diuine meditation profitable for all Christians to knowe and practice; exemplified with a large meditation of eternall life*.[2] As rules of monastic life were inherently aimed at conformity and obedience to an order of practice and place that required uniformity, one did not join an

---

1. Senn, *Protestant Spiritual Traditions*, 170.
2. Huntley, *Bishop Joseph Hall*, 65–118. Hall's text is included in this volume in its 1633 publication and will be the primary source used in this study.

order to freelance. This rigidity was the feature of monastic submission, as the *Rule of St. Benedict* implied.³ Hall's approach allowed freedom and flexibility, ever attentive to the needs and conditions of the average parishioner. In substance, Hall's *Art* provided *not more* restrictions on the role of the imagination but greater freedom to use the senses, the faculties of the soul, and the intellect that would have deep relevance for a Protestant spirituality and an English aesthetic. This is one major thesis of this study. A Puritan imagination is one full of creative possibilities. Ironically, this would make Hall more medieval in substance than the Counter-Reformation models, which reflected more modern assumptions and hints towards an Enlightenment view of the soul.⁴ It is a central argument that counters the traditional view that Ignatian spirituality was a framework that placed the imagination in a positive and active role in the shaping of the soul in the image of Christ. While not renouncing all the ways sensory epistemology was affirmed in the use of the Jesuits, this thesis affirms that many Puritans, and especially the foundational work of Hall, provided a more robust view of the imagination that was open to a wide variety of opinions and a multifaceted view of reality. As this chapter seeks to give extensive commentary on Hall's method and his steps, his approach with its distinctions from Ignatian views and his continuity with ancient traditions will become evident. There are hints of his objective in the opening of his dedicatory page.

The first edition was published with a foreword to Sir Richard Lea. This indicated that this manual was not written as a specialized guide for the monastic religious life but for the ordinary lay person. Hall began by detailing the importance of meditation for every believer. "This alone is the remedy of security and worldliness, the pastime of saints, the ladder of heaven, and, in short, the best improvement of Christianity. Learn it who can and neglect who list; he shall never find joy neither in God nor in himself which doth not both know and practice it."⁵ The introduction contained the familiar discussion of the types of meditation and their value. A unique contribution of Hall is the discussion of occasional meditation, or what he called "extemporal meditation." While *The Art of Meditation* was not aimed primarily at this type, he presented it as a valuable and important part of spiritual progress.

---

3. Benedict, *Rule of St. Benedict*, 19: ". . . faithfully observing his [God's] teaching in the monastery until death . . ."

4. There were two schools of thought at the University of Paris in the time of Gerson which become more pronounced in the colleges of the university during the days of Calvin and Ignatius of Loyola.

5. Huntley, *Bishop Joseph Hall*, 71.

MODEL AND METHOD

The place that occasional meditation had among later Puritans and its implications for the complexity of how the imagination was utilized will be detailed in chapter 5 on the faculties of the soul. The philosophical sources for the terminology and development of thought on theological anthropology sheds light on how many Puritans understood the complexity of soul, mind, and will and the nature of the imagination. There the background on the relationship of the imagination to other functions of the soul in relation to epistemology and the senses will be placed in the context of Hall's overall work. It is noteworthy to state that the Jesuit model did little to promote occasional meditation.[6] Before Hall wrote his *Art* he had published a book of meditations which were meditations on everyday events: *Meditations and Vows* (1603). His later work entitled *Occasional Meditations* was published in 1630 and contains many short entries of contemplations of common things in the natural world which Hall connects to spiritual truths. We find in him a love for good things in the world and not an asceticism of rejecting the good and beautiful aspects of God's creation nor shunning the work of recreating beauty in the hands of his image bearers. Hall reflected a love for music, as indicated by one of his chapters.

In the chapter entitled "Upon the Hearing of a Lute Well Played On," he writes:

> There may be (for ought we know) infinite inventions of art the possibility whereof we should hardly ever believe if they were fore-reported to us . . . only by an hollow piece of wood and the guts of beasts stirred by the fingers of men, to make so sweet and melodious a noise, we should have thought it utterly incredible; yet now that we see and hear it ordinarily done we make it no wonder. It is no marvel if we cannot fore-imagine what kind and means of harmony God will have used by his saints and angels in heaven, when these poor matters seem so strange to our conceits which, yet our very senses are convinced of. Oh God, Thou knowest infinite ways to glorify Thyself by the creatures which do far transcend our weak and finite capacities. Let me wonder

---

6. This difference is more than stylistic, but rather critical in how both systems operated from different philosophical categories. The Ignatian model is based on passages of Scripture and filled with reflection on the life of Christ, hence it appears to be free of extrabiblical and philosophical adornments. Yet the system, as this work argues, is tied to some assumptions about the soul and the imaginations which determines the affections to be more modern in its epistemology. The influence of the Averroes's view of Aristotle, tilted toward a bifurcated rationalism, is a strong possibility, for the reasoning faculty plays a higher role among the Jesuits.

at Thy wisdom and power and be more aweful in my adoration than curious in my inquirers.[7]

The lute in the hands of a gifted musician, for Hall, turned not to mental curiosity or aesthetic interest alone but to a contemplation that called a soul to wonder within a sense of awe at the beauty of the Creator. The organ of hearing was transformed to a means of awareness that the beauty of music was a dim reflection of a greater music that transcended the earthly experience. Occasional meditation was a key element of the use of the imagination for a redemptive and sanctifying purpose. This was a major theme running throughout the devotional writings of Hall, hence this trajectory of applying the imagination was a central concept to this positive work of piety. In chapter 6, this study will return to the issue of the way Hall's use of occasional meditation was carried on in the Protestant tradition in England.

The Art of Meditation was directed to the intentional kind of meditation, in giving a framework that supported both kinds of approaches to meditation. This guide's flexible nature was aimed at being both suitable and adaptable to the needs of a broad spectrum of parishioners. Yet it was rooted in a tradition that exhibited medieval piety and acted as a translator of this spiritual practice for a new audience. In his preliminary notes at the beginning, he used a common initiatory discussion of the need to confess sin and to prepare the soul for this spiritual course. "The hill of meditation may not be climbed with a profane food; but as in the delivery of the Law, so here no beast may touch God's hill lest he die; only the pure of heart have promise to see God [Matt 5:8] . . . Whereupon not unfitly did that worthy Chancellor of Paris make the first stair of his ladder of contemplation humble repentance."[8]

Following the model of Jean Gerson and the medieval tradition of purgation, he affirmed the need to confess and turn from sin. In contrast to the Ignatian model, which is intended as a thirty-day retreat, the first two weeks are spent in confession and purgation. Hall placed confession of sin as part of the preparatory steps of clearing the mind and preparing the heart. There is no time and specific requirements, but only helps and guides in *The Art*. A brief outline is shown here of his preliminary chapters which prepared a person in the preparation of entering into meditation:

1. Confession of sin—clearing the heart.
2. Freeing from worldly thoughts—clearing the mind.
3. Discipline/routine.

---

7. Hall, *Occasional Meditation*, 167.
8. Huntley, *Bishop Joseph Hall*, 75. Here we see Hall making a reference to Gerson.

Preliminary Practical Issues

1. Find the right place (uninterrupted sacred space).
2. Set a time.
3. Place and posture of body.
    a. Begin with prayer.
    b. Choosing the object of meditation (personal freedom).

As the meditation on the lute suggests, Hall's model provides a large degree of freedom and the work of the Spirit in both the Bible and the world are places where the imagination can be engaged in divine realities. Ignatian practice is not flexible in this regard outside the selections of the life of Christ. Hall does not dismiss the value of Scripture or the life and work of Christ; he just enlarges the scope of how meditation can be applied.

THE METHOD

As Bishop Hall moved into the part of his guide that contains the actual steps, it is obvious that he kept the rules rather brief and simple in comparison to the Ignatian model. As the noted historian Ozment makes clear,

> The *SE* built most perceptively on the interconnection of emotion, belief, and behavior. What justification by faith had attempted to accomplish for the anguished Protestant saint, Ignatius's disciplined exercises tried to do for the troubled Catholic saint. The routines it prescribed overcame old habits and prepared individuals for new states of mind and morality by playing directly on their basic emotions of fear and love. Particular sins, for example, were eliminated by attacking each with all five senses and the mind's power of imagination at regular daily intervals.[9]

The goal for Hall was not merely to roll over ideas in the mind as a scholastic, but to enliven the affections for the lover of God, whether in a shop, field, or study. The steps in meditation began with cognitive reasoning, but they end with the heart longing and delighting in the presence of God. "Entering into meditation should follow an order. It begins in the understanding and ends in the affections; it begins in the brain and descends to the heart; begins on earth, ascends to heaven, not suddenly but by certain stairs and degrees till we come to the highest."[10] Using the language of ascent whether

---

9. Ozment, *Age of Reform*, 412.
10. Huntley, *Bishop Joseph Hall*, 87.

it be a mountain or a "interior castle,"[11] a ladder or stairs, the same idea is expressed. Developing an often-ignored part of Calvin's theology, Julie Canlis puts forth a constructive ascetic theology in Calvin. She notes this tradition of piety in saying:

> St. Denis—and John Climacus saw the steps upward as ascent, but also inward as in descent, both were used to describe the soul's progress . . . The concept of ascent in the understanding's role of moving through the spiritual process of turning from sin . . . the descent is where the affections are engaged towards greater love. We find the concept readily in the fourth century, such as St. Gregory of Nazianzus and St. John Chrysostom . . . and Theodoret of Cyrus in the fifth, had already spoken of the spiritual life as a ladder, up which by God's grace we mount step by step.[12]

John's *Ladder* has thirty steps which correspond to the earthly life of Jesus. His work is divided into two books. The first book is on preparing the soul through reflecting on sin and the need for divine grace. The section book is a guide to reflecting on the life of Christ, which corresponds to the soul's journey towards fuller experience of the divine life. Like Hall's *Art*, this Eastern manual was written to apply to the layperson as well as the cloistered monk. Sometimes he is referred to as St. John of the Ladder, a beloved writer in the Eastern Orthodox tradition.[13] A defined process is needed to maximize one's success in the endeavor. But for this method, the rules were not meant to confine or dictate the journey, but to be a helpful guide along the way. Finding the right place, away from distractions, the time and posture is also considered. There is a freedom and stress on the needs and situation of the individual in Hall's approach that is a highlight of practical and pastoral sensitivity. Here is a simple outline of his steps in meditation:

Scale of Meditation

1. Question—What should I think about?
2. Excussion (Possession)—What I should take hold of and what should I reject and not think on?

---

11. Medwick, *Teresa of Avila*, 206. The model used by Teresa was different than a ladder or mountain, as she describes: "Well then, let's imagine that this castle has—as I've said—many chambers, some above, others below and at the sides, and in the very center, the middle of all the rest, is the most important one, which is where the most secret exchanges take place between God and the soul."
12. Canlis, *Calvin's Ladder*.
13. Climacus, *Ladder of Divine Ascent*, 11.

3. Decision of topic.

4. Commemoration (Remembrance)—Recalling from memory about the subject.

5. Consideration—or revolving the mind over the subject.

6. Attention—A focused area and fastening it in the mind.

7. Explanation—Clearing of the subject by similitudes.

8. Tractation (Application)—Extending the focus into other areas of life.

9. Dijudication (Discernment)—estimation of the worth of the subject above other things.

10. Causation—Confirmation of the estimation of the worth.[14]

SOURCE THEORIES: MEDIEVAL ENGLISH TEXTS

Before the discussion of the division of steps that Hall described, it is important to describe in historical development various models of the ladders of ascent in medieval mysticism. It has been suggested that Hall's method was not very practical and too obtuse to be of much influence on subsequent Protestant piety. In total, Hall outlined eighteen steps and broke them down into two sections, in a similar way found in both Walter Hilton and John of Climacus. Reading through his own *Art* in comparison with other medieval models, it will be apparent that Hall was simplifying this tradition for his audience. He did this in two ways. First, his text was far shorter than others, and dispensed with other rules of the monastic tradition rooted in both a Benedictine order and the rules of his contemporary Jesuits. Secondly, Hall provided a model of both ascent and descent, where climbing up the mountain of spiritual bliss called for a descent back to the world. This aspect was not so unique to Hall, but it conveyed the careful interaction of piety with worldly engagement. Hall's steps were also not a required rule that must be followed in order to properly engage the affections. Repeatedly, Hall reminded his readers that the steps can be skipped and shortened depending on the needs of the person and the subject of the meditation.

---

14. Hall, *Art*, 51. The ten steps are in light of the complexity of medieval rules and its sheer length is a comparatively simple approach, although Hall's method would be simplified even further by men such as Thomas Watson. This can't be understood as anything other than following Hall's methodology of simplification for practical reasons.

PREPARATION FOR DELIBERATE MEDITATION: PURGATION

He cannot proceed through contemplation to the heavenly Jerusalem unless he goes through the blood of the Lamb as through a gate.

—St. Bonaventure

First, the qualification of the person who meditates is to be free from sin; hence the first step was purgation from sin. In common with monastic practice, it was humiliation or self-abasement that rightly proceeded to an admission of sin. "The hill of meditation may not be climbed with a profane foot."[15] Sin is a distraction and an encumbrance that will keep meditation from moving upward to the glories of eternal realities. "Sin dimmeth and dazzleth the eye, that it cannot behold spiritual things."[16] Purgation was a well-known concept among medieval authors and spiritual practices. Hall incorporated this as a feature that Protestants could embrace. "The soul must therefore be purged ere it can profitable meditate."[17] The biblical example of David was given: "I will wash my hands in innocency, then I will compass thy altar" (Ps 26:6).[18] The use of the penitential verses in the Scriptures, especially from the Psalms, has been seen in the history of the Christian church. The way of purgation was simply another way to speak about repentance and the turning from sin. For example, it was in the Hebrides revival (1950s) that Psalm 24 was such a catalyst for the outpouring of the Spirit:

> Who shall ascend into the hill of the LORD? or who shall stand in his holy place? He that hath clean hands, and a pure heart; who hath not lifted up his soul unto vanity, nor sworn deceitfully. He shall receive the blessing from the LORD, and righteousness from the God of his salvation. This is the generation of them that seek him, that seek thy face, O Jacob. Selah.[19]

---

15. Huntley, *Bishop Joseph Hall*, 75.
16. Huntley, *Bishop Joseph Hall*, 75.
17. Huntley, *Bishop Joseph Hall*, 76.
18. Huntley, *Bishop Joseph Hall*, 76.
19. Psalm 24:3–6. Evan Roberts, whom God used in a mighty way to usher in the great Welsh revival of the early twentieth century that led to over hundred thousand conversions, would also use the Psalms. Ian J. Shaw records the impact of that revival in his *Churches, Revolutions, and Empires*, 514.

This psalm was used in the prologue of the *Rule of St. Benedict* as a way of preparing the novice for a right heart.[20] There are not many citations of historical sources in this work, but here Hall mentioned his principal guide: "That worthy chancellor of Paris [Gerson] make the first stair of his ladder of contemplation humble repentance."[21] It is humility which was the foundation of the double knowledge of God—*duplex cognition Dei*[22] defined in Calvin's prologue of his *Institutes* and also expressed by Bernard of Clairvaux:

> When men know themselves in the light of truth and so think less of themselves, it will certainly follow that what they loved before will now become bitter to them. They are brought face to face with themselves and blush at what they see. Their present state is no pleasure to them. They aspire to something better and, at the same time, realize how little they can rely on themselves to achieve it. It hurts them, and they find some relief in judging themselves severely. Love of truth makes them hunger and thirst after justice [Matt 5:6] and conceive a deep contempt for themselves ... They fly from justice to mercy.[23]

This reflected a rich understanding that what lays behind a true evangelical humility was a God of grace, not a self-imposed hatred of the self or despising of the soul. Purgation in the theological context of free grace and imputed justification was not the human attempt to remove the stain of original sin or the trace of all ongoing sin. Hall stated clearly that "absolute perfection" is not the requirement here, but "rather an honest sincerity of the heart, not willingly sinning, willingly repenting when we have sinned."[24]

---

20. Benedict, *Rule of St. Benedict*, Prologue 22–33. This edition cites Psalm 14, which has similar wording and thinking to Psalm 24, and the Trappist monk Merton believes it is Psalm 24. This does not change the basic biblical concern of the need for purity. Merton states, "This same Psalm is one of the cornerstones of monastic spirituality, since it has an important place in the Prologue to St. Benedict's Rule. It is therefore interesting to see how much a monastic saint like Bernard of Clairvaux could find in it. He notes these lines in the Psalm, reflecting the thought, 'the Fathers believed "purity of heart" to be a function of that gift of understanding, which is one of the keys to mystical contemplation'" (Merton, *Bread in the Wilderness*, 104).

21. Huntley, *Bishop Joseph Hall*, 75. Here we see Hall making a reference to Gerson.

22. Muller, *Dictionary of Latin and Greek Theological Terms*, 99. This natural knowledge does not imply it is available apart from redemptive saving knowledge but shows how they both work together. Richard Muller explains, Protestant orthodoxy drew on natural theology as a basis or foundation on which to build a body of Christian doctrine.

23. Sommerfeldt, *Bernard of Clairvaux*, 55–56.

24. Huntley, *Bishop Joseph Hall*, 76.

Neither should the task of purging provide an obstacle for those who would embark on this spiritual path. Hall saw meditation as spiritual medicine, not as a high-velocity workout for those already spiritually fit. Those who sin and know it have no excuse not to meditate, but instead have a reason to, as Hall explained: "simple man . . . being half starved with cold, refuseth to come near the fire, because he findeth not heat enough in himself."[25]

Meditation was not the exclusive fruit of the skilled expert climber but an invitation to the weak and the yearning to find sustenance and health for their souls. The process of purgation was rooted in true repentance. Richard Baxter in 1696 reflected on the individual way the Holy Spirit brings conviction, stating, "But I understood at last that God breaketh not all men's hearts alike."[26] So the process of purgation and repentance was not a one-size-fits-all but required a particular and singular focus on the individual heart. Hall suggested, "And as of old they were wont to search for and thrust out malefactors from the presence ere they went to sacrifice, so must we our sins ere we offer our thoughts to God."[27]

The seventh-century Syrian monk John Climacus referred to repentance as "a contract with God for a fresh start in life. Repentance goes shopping for humility. Repentance is critical awareness and is the daughter of hope and the refusal to despair."[28] Hall's style of writing and use of imagery is remarkably close to that of this Eastern father. Indeed, Hall understood that purgation was pregnant with hopeful confidence of divine mercy and a call to climb the summit.

Secondly, after purgation the one who meditated should seek to leave behind all worldly thoughts. Clearly, Hall understood worldly thoughts as the cares and demands of this life, not a world-denying asceticism. "Cares are a heavy load and uneasy; these must be laid down at the bottom of this hill if we ever look to attain the top."[29] It is Hall's point towards an understanding that meditation was not a monistic/pantheistic approach of reaching all thoughtlessness, but a singleness of mind, what is called "mindfulness."[30] "When one thinks upon many things, then we think of nothing";[31] according to Hall, the mind can become restless if left unbridled to the cares of this

---

25. Huntley, *Bishop Joseph Hall*, 76.
26. Baxter, *Religquiae Basterianae*, I.7, in Beougher, *Richard Baxter and Conversion*, 77.
27. Huntley, *Bishop Joseph Hall*, 75.
28. Climacus, *Ladder of Divine Ascent*, 121.
29. Huntley, *Bishop Joseph Hall*, 51.
30. Mindfulness defined here as single-focused. The author of the *Cloud of Unknowing* states it as, "Active life is troubled and travailed about many things; but contemplative sitteth in peace with one thing" (Underhill, *Cloud of Unknowing*, 18).
31. Huntley, *Bishop Joseph Hall*, 76.

life. Cognitive reasoning is not devalued or dismissed, but the engagement of the emotive and pre-thinking aspect of the soul is brought to balance in a focused way. As the philosopher Kierkegaard wrote, "Singleness of mind is to will one thing," so preparation for meditation requires an effort to move towards a particular truth to contemplate its fullness. Hall made it clear what must be done:

> Neither may the soul that hopeth to profit by meditation suffer itself for the time entangled with the world, which is all one as to come to God's flaming bush on the hill of visions with our shoes on our feet [Exod 3:2–3]. Thou seest the bird whose feathers are limed unable to take her former flight; so are we when our thoughts are clinged together by the world [unable] to soar up to our heaven in meditation . . . It must be a free and a light mind that can ascend this mount of contemplation, overcoming this height, this steepness.[32]

The words of Hall echoed the teaching of John Climacus on prayer; "The beginning of prayer is the expulsion of distractions from the very start by a single thought . . . Faith gives wings to prayer, and without it no one can fly upward to heaven."[33] It was not a pantheistic emptying of the understanding, but a singleness of focus through the dependence upon faith. The parallel between these two writers, separated by centuries, is stunning; arguably there is a connection. The fact is that Puritans such as William Perkins claimed that the first few centuries of the church were in line with the antiquity of the English Protestant faith. Anthony Milton argues this valid succession with the pre-Reformation church of the East and the English Church.[34]

Thirdly, in the preliminary stage of preparation, the meditator should be constant in both time and matter. As a spiritual discipline and in distinction from the previously mentioned occasional meditation, this intentional and deliberate approach should have a regular pattern in one's day. Hall believed in the cultivation of holy habits; therefore there should be "a set course and hour reserved for this work."[35] Recognizing that we are creatures of habit, the daily regimen of taking time for eating usually has a set time. Like daily meals, Hall encouraged, "Thus feed thy soul by meditation. Set

---

32. Huntley, *Bishop Joseph Hall*, 76.

33. Climacus, *Ladder of Divine Ascent*, 276–77.

34. Milton, *Catholic and Reformed*, 272–73. Elsewhere he notes, "the Jacobean period witnessed a concerted effort by many divines to claim fellowship with the Eastern churches which had never fallen under the direct control of the Latin Church" (Milton, *Catholic and Reformed*, 379).

35. Huntley, *Bishop Joseph Hall*, 77.

thine hours and keep them . . . there is no hardness in this practice but in the beginning."³⁶ Included are practical tips for when disrupted or even when a time was missed, to keep the task the next day—pay oneself back, in other words, for lost time. Ever before Hall was a pragmatism that steered clear of a dogmatic rigor of rules.

There is one category that Hall took an exception to this liberty, hence a word of warning was given that regular and daily meditation was necessary for clergy and those in charge of the care of souls:

> For thou shalt find that deferring breeds (besides the loss) an indisposition to good; so that what was before pleasant to thee being omitted, tomorrow grows harsh, the next day unnecessary, afterwards odious . . . Those whose very trade is Divinity (methinks) should omit no day without their line of meditation. Those which are secular men, not many, remembering that they have a common calling of Christianity to attend as well as a special vocation in the world, and that other being more noble and important, may justly challenge both often and diligent service.³⁷

There is an important feature of this discipline that underlined Hall's emphasis on meditation being a regular and constant practice. Hall saw meditation as necessary for all believers in the progress of sanctification, but he did not impose a rule or strict guidelines for the way about doing it. But his freedom is not meant as to excuse a lackadaisical attitude of this practice, especially for clergy. There is indeed a balance between form and freedom. The idea of flexible use of time, yet within a fixed and regular habit is also seen in the English and Augustinian tradition and the unknown author of *The Cloud of Unknowing*; "In one little time, as little as it is, may heaven be won and lost. A token it is that time is precious: for God, that is given of time, giveth never two times together, but each one after other. And this He doth, for He will not reverse the order or the ordinal course in the cause of His creation. For time is made for man, and not man for time."³⁸

The role of habit is what begins to create the environment of soul care. It is the *habitus fidei*³⁹ where inclination is born and cultivated by expe-

---

36. Huntley, *Bishop Joseph Hall*, 77.
37. Huntley, *Bishop Joseph Hall*, 77–78.
38. Underhill, *Cloud of Unknowing*, 9.
39. Muller, *Dictionary of Latin and Greek Theological Terms*, 146. He states that this is "the God-given spiritual capacity of fallen human beings to have faith: i.e., if the mind and will are not disposed to have faith, faith is impossible . . . the human being will not come to faith unless the *habitus fides* is once again instilled." As this a gift from God, the *habitus gratiae* is the ongoing "disposition for knowing . . . for something to be received by the mind, will or affections, there must be a resident disposition, or *habitus*, present to

rience and behavior. One is to learn this habit of the heart—to shape the soul, for as Hall mentioned throughout this work, the benefit is not just a spiritual climb to a summit as an end to itself, but a twofold blessing: deeper knowledge of the self and of God—*duplex cognito*. In chapter 5, this discussion of the two knowledges will be detailed in a way that Hall would use his source material. From Augustine to Bernard of Clairvaux and John Calvin, the concept of self-knowing has an integral component and theology in contemplative prayer and meditation. The importance at the present is to see how Hall was importing this tradition in his preparation on meditation and his Augustinian/Calvinistic view of faith.

St. Bonaventure (1221–74), Franciscan theologian and Bishop of Abano, known as the Seraphic Doctor, wrote about the order of the soul and saw a similar connection of these two knowledges. According to F. Copleston, "Man's spiritual assent means a turning from the 'shadow' or more remote likeness to the 'image of God' and from the image to the exemplary cause itself, that is, to God."[40] This movement towards knowing God moves beyond the possessing of certain benefits of cognitive truths about God or the personal acquisition of spiritual maturity but moves towards the contemplation of God for its own sake. The movement and transition from being mere travelers exploring a foreign land to finding our true home or rediscovering our true habitation, regaining paradise on earth. This was done not by idleness but a holy stillness and being present in the moment, not in a sense of quietism but in a focus on the one object of contemplation, as "this constancy requires of thee to keep day with thyself unless thou wilt prove bankrupt in good exercises, so also that thy mind should dwell upon the same thought without flitting, without weariness, until it have attained to some issue of spiritual profit."[41] Holy habits are acquired through constancy of practice and with the skill that is honed by practice. Hall's earlier work featuring the idea of traveling to an unknown country may be in the background of his analogy where travelers were distinguished from native dwellers.[42] Hall's emphasis is always to stress the inward journey of

---

receive it" (Muller, *Dictionary of Latin and Greek Theological Terms*, 146). In Hall's view, the use of meditation is not an infusion of grace, but the outworking of our justification and the gift of grace expressed in our longing to love God, who has loved us.

40. Copleston, *Medieval Philosophy*, 76.

41. Huntley, *Bishop Joseph Hall*, 78.

42. Wands, *Another World and Yet the Same*. A dystopian novel filled with satire and perhaps a warning against the dangers of travels to lands of corrupt morals, one can argue that Hall's invitation to travel in the path of heavenly contemplation is an inward journey towards renewing the soul. The question this raises is one that argues for the Protestant version, indeed patristic version (as indicated by John Climacus, for pilgrims to find their own spiritual Sinai) of spiritual pilgrimage.

a spiritual pilgrimage rather than as tourists who saw distant worlds in a superficial manner. "Those that do only travel through Africa become not blackamoors; but those which are born there, those that inhabit there."[43] The art of this discipline was not just to equip the traveler in unknown territory, but to provide a sense of being. "The mind of man is of a strange metal; if it be not used, it rusteth."[44]

Habitus fides is the concept described by Aquinas as the inner condition of the heart that provided the environment for grace to enliven the will to direct the intellect or rational faculty of the soul. This was in continuity with the Dominican idea of combining the works of piety with the labors of everyday life. Hall affirmed the habit of the monastic orders who combined prayer and manual work. One sees the similar striving for moderation in the Hilton's *Scale of Perfection*. Hall alluded to this Benedictine balance: "those ancient monks who intermeddled bodily labour with their contemplations proved so excellent in this divine business."[45] This way avoided the problems of a speculative mysticism that sought to bypass the physical world and the mind. Hall was critical of those monastic orders that "spend wholly upon their beads and crucifix, pretending no other work but meditation, have cold hearts to God, and to the world show nothing but a dull shadow of devotion."[46] There was in Hall's approach an awareness of the danger of relying upon a method in mechanical rote usage that disregarded true engagement with the soul and the affections. Neither was there in Hall a requirement for times and duration strictly defined. There was an intentional flexibility where the focus is not on the hour of the day or the length of the devotion but a growing practice, as Hall wrote, "making always not our hour-glass, but some competent increase in our devotion, the measure of our continuance."[47]

In the monastic tradition, the role of contemplative prayer gave monks and nuns the ability to preserve more of the day for this practice. This was not rejected by Hall, as he commended a major source, Jean Gerson, the chancellor of the University of Paris; "Gerson (saving our just quarrel against him for the Council of Constance), I rather use because our adversaries disclaim him for theirs, professeth he hath been sometimes four hours together

---

43. Huntley, *Bishop Joseph Hall*, 78.
44. Huntley, *Bishop Joseph Hall*, 78.
45. Huntley, *Bishop Joseph Hall*, 54.
46. Huntley, *Bishop Joseph Hall*, 54.
47. Huntley, *Bishop Joseph Hall*, 54. The monastic rule of set hours is rooted in a regimen of set times for all the monks under the authority of the abbot. Its very nature required conformity to times and schedules. Hall opens the practice to those of various callings and vocations in a manner that was inclusive of the whole Christian community.

working his heart ere he could frame it to purpose."[48] This citation reveals Hall's ability to reference sources for certain theological points, but with an eye towards discernment and contextual adaptation. For those in vocations restricted to secular duties and domestic responsibilities, Hall counseled the souls applying his method to "persist therefore, and prevail" in the ascent to the mountain of communion with God.[49] This was piety for the practical and the common life, not an ironclad method for the religious life.

THE PLACE AND TIME OF MEDITATION: SACRED OF THE ORDINARY

Keeping in mind that so far Hall was dealing with just the preliminaries of meditation, he offered a variety of options that equipped a person involved in this practice. These are meant to prepare and provide guidelines to create the atmosphere and right approach to meditation. Referring to "ancient counsel of a great master of this art," there are three necessary things related to the place and environment conducive to good meditation: secrecy, silence, and rest. One needs to be alone, so seeking solitude where one can be without interruption. Then one is to remove all noise and sounds of the world, which would mean the typical distractions of a busy day, not the natural sounds of a river, birds, or a spring breeze among the trees. The discipline of stillness is not so much about avoiding motion, for Hall indicated a preference for walking while meditating, as in movement there was a stillness of the soul: "Be still and know that I am God" (Ps 46:10).

Hall indicated that for some reason there was usually one place where out of habit and custom we find God to be nearer to us than other places. This idea of sacred space was not elaborated nor specified regarding typical religious spaces, as one might assume of a churchman and a Conformist. An altar can be found in a garden, and a chapel might be a simple clearing in the woods near one's home. Sacred space was defined by personal circumstances and needs, not so much by ecclesiastical determination. This regular place of solitude was recommended as a place of regular meditation. Belden Lane notes how the Puritans of New England incorporated this notion: "Look on the world, urged John Cotton, as 'a mappe and shadow of the spiritual estate of the soules of men.' The landscape served as a catechist, carefully drilling the catechumen in lessons of the holy."[50] Hall would agree

---

48. Huntley, *Bishop Joseph Hall*, 54.
49. Huntley, *Bishop Joseph Hall*, 55.
50. Lane, *Landscapes of the Sacred*, 104. See also Lane, *Ravished by Beauty*.

that solitary places provide a geographic space for the soul to be receptive and engaged, as seen in this passage:

> Solitariness of place is fittest for meditation. Retire thyself from others if thou wouldst talk profitable with thyself. So Jesus meditates alone in the Mount, Isaac in the fields, John the Baptist in the desert, David on his bed [Ps 4:4], Chrysostom in his bath, each in several places but solitary. There is no place free from God, not to which He is more tied. One finds his closet most convenient, where his eyes, being limited by the known walls, call in the mind after a sort from wandering abroad. Another findeth his soul more free when it beholdeth his heaven above and about him. It matters not so we be solitary and silent. It was a witty and divine speech of Bernard, that the spouse of the soul, Christ Jesus, is bashful, neither willingly cometh to his Bride in the presence of a multitude.[51]

Not only place but time was also considered. No fixed time was prescribed, but Hall indicated that for most the mornings were fit. "No precept, no practice of others, can be prescribed to us in this circumstance."[52] In matters of the time and hours, the rule was not regulated by any controls other than that which was determined by the individual choice of the pilgrim. This principle holds true for the variety of postures that can be best suited for this art.

Understanding that the soul was part of the body and interconnected in intellect, will, and feelings, Hall referred to different postures the body can use in meditating. Hence, "site and gesture of the body" speak more about how a person oriented their body on a meditation.[53] Again, Hall did not prescribe a set pattern of posturing the body. He mentioned the guides and examples of Jean Gerson, Guliel (William of Paris or William of St. Theirry[54]), and Dionys Carthus[55] to show the variation that existed in the use of the body. The advice of either sitting and looking heavenward or leaning towards the left with rest for the heart and another standing with eyes closed

---

51. Huntley, *Bishop Joseph Hall*, 80.
52. Huntley, *Bishop Joseph Hall*, 56.
53. Huntley, *Bishop Joseph Hall*, 82.
54. Huntley, *Bishop Joseph Hall*, 203. Huntley believes this Guiliel of Paris (many worthies have the same name) is the fourteenth-century mystic of the Dominican monastery of Jacques de Paris. A probable source may be William of St. Thierry, a student of Abelard and of the same tradition as St. Bernard. William's notable work *On Contemplating God* is, in the view of this author, a likely influence upon Hall and fits with the same trajectory of sources that he is linking together.
55. Dionys Carthus is Dionysius, sometimes referred to in English texts as St. Denis.

to the heavens were not meant to be prescribed models but examples of the freedom of application. Hall personally preferred the way of Isaac, who, as Scripture recorded, meditated while he walked in a field (Gen 24:63).

In this way, the mind, senses, and the body are fully engaged in the imagination, not cut off from the world of God's creation. Hence, the use of the body, while allowing for the freedom of the practitioner to follow what's best for his/her disposition, affirmed the relationship of the body to the soul.[56] "In all which the body, as it is the instrument and vassal of the soul, so will easily follow the affections."[57] As the "vassal" of the soul, Hall's view of the body was both positive and essential in the engagement of meditation with both eyes closed or open, either in a closet or a wooded field. The soul needs space and context, just as the body provides contours for the faculties of the soul, our physical environment shapes our spiritual imagination.

HUMANS ARE MEDITATIO CREATURAS

On the matter and subject of meditation, Hall argued that all persons meditate. The pressing concern for Hall was what subject one will meditate and why that subject was selected. Humans are in essence *mediatio creaturas*, Hall explained: "We all meditate: one, how to do ill to others; another, how to do some earthly good to himself; another . . . as how to accomplish his lewd desires . . . how he may sin unseen."[58] Our created soul was embodied to look towards our God, as reflecting the divine image which yearns for restoration. But the inward predisposition without the grace of God can only create a false shadow of what it truly longs to attain. Souls damaged by original sin are not able to mediate, no matter how beneficial meditation is for the body or for natural spiritual nourishment. Hence, while many spiritual traditions, Jesuits included, can recount the various benefits of meditation, this for Hall is not definitive of authentic spiritual meditation upon God through divine grace. In a sense, meditating is reasonably a natural inclination of the human soul. It is as though our hearts are bent towards the "vain imaginations" of sinful and selfish ends, yet our faces are heavenward. Even when meditating on the natural world, a person can admire the order and wonder of what he/she sees but draw no special benefit of knowing

---

56. Hall was also concerned with too much focus on the body or externals in its impact on the affections. This was true also for Underhill, *Cloud of Unknowing*, 102: "If they be done by the stirring of the spirit, then be they well done, and else be thy hypocrisy, and then be they false."

57. Huntley, *Bishop Joseph Hall*, 58.

58. Huntley, *Bishop Joseph Hall*, 58.

the interior of the heart. One can enter contemplation merely as a natural activity and be drawn even to things unprofitable or sinful as the English mystic and author of *The Cloud of Unknowing* warned, "the devil hath his contemplatives."[59] What is needed is the ability to think and ponder about godly and eternal subjects in a renewed heart. As the apostle Paul reminded his readers, "While we look not at the things which are seen, but at the things which are not seen: for the things which are seen are temporal; but the things that are not seen are eternal" (2 Cor 4:18).

Ignatius placed in his method certain topics and events in the life of Christ. Hall listed a rather lengthy set of ideas on subjects worthy of meditation in addition to the work and ministry of Jesus Christ. There was a sense that meditating on objects or events the objective was not to rest in the external truths but the utilization of these subjects/objects, pointing to a greater devotion and love for God. Hall included in list a warning regarding a faulty use of contemplation, even objects seemingly good and spiritual. Events in the life of Christ and his passion, as well as doctrinal truths about divinity and human sinfulness and the dangers of hell, are all meant to posture the soul towards greater affection toward God.[60] Thinking upon truths of Scripture without the affections being inflamed with love of God can be a useless activity, even though it may have the external appearance of godliness.

THE STEPS IN MEDITATION

Next, Hall moved to the demonstration of the actual practice of meditation. The foregone discussion being on the level of practical preliminaries, the next part of Hall's work is the central structure of the ascent up the mountain towards greater experience in God's love. Hall's division of a threefold pattern follows an old tradition of this medieval triad: entrance, proceeding, and conclusion. It was the grammar of monastic learning that was aimed at the whole person. Going back to Augustine and St. Gregory, it was a sacred learning and listening to God. Jean Lecercq notes, "This way of uniting reading, meditation and prayer, this 'meditative prayer' as William of St.

---

59. Underhill, *Cloud of Unknowing*, 80–99. There are repeated warnings in this work that provide warning about the dangers of speculations and not having the mind engaged rightly on divine realities. The many times the text warns of dangers reflects this Augustinian grasp of human proclivity towards idolatry. "Insomuch that oftentimes the devil feigneth quaint sounds in their ears . . . and all is but falsehood" (Underhill, *Cloud of Unknowing*, 99). Physical eyes, ears, and smells may seem to be reliable receptors of truth, but the author, like Hall, understands this can be manipulated and distorted.

60. Huntley, *Bishop Joseph Hall*, 58.

Thierry calls it, 'had great influence on religious psychology.'"[61] This was similar to Luther's division of the spiritual practice of *oratio, meditatio,* and *tentatio*—prayer, meditation, and application.[62] The tradition was steeped in an Augustinian approach to spiritual contemplation and the anonymous English mystic. A tradition well known by Hall, he would refer to it as "Lesson, Meditation and Orison."[63] That the reading of Scripture is not specified by Hall did not mean he suggested a model that dispensed with the priority of God's Word in one's approach to God. Scripture is to be a regular part of a daily diet and the mind filled with the Bible's content as the basis of thinking about God. "We fools, when will we be wise, and turning our eyes from vanity, with that sweet singer of Israel, make God's statues our song and meditation in the house of our pilgrimage."[64]

PRAYER AND MEDITATION: A SYNTHESIS

First, the entrance to meditation was *oratio* or prayer. Some think that meditation was the preparation for prayer, but Hall, who followed Bernard, thought it was prayer that prepared one for the work of meditation. "Prayer is our speech to God, says Bernard. Meditation is God's speech to the heart; the heart must speak to God, that God may speak to it."[65] Here was the great key to understanding how Hall appropriates meditation as inner experiential knowledge of God within the soul. It worked in the soul as an incubator of faith, not in a semi-Pelagian effort but in response to God's work of grace. "Faith," said Augustine, "since it is a thing of the heart, not of the body; nor is it without apart from us, but deeply seated within us."[66] While prayer engages the intellect it also prepares the inner soul for longings and "groanings that cannot be uttered" (Rom 8:26). Augustine described this as interconnected between two kinds of knowing in the soul:

> For as holy contemplation has two forms of ecstasy, one in the intellect, the other in the will [*in intellectu unus et alter in affect*]; one of the enlightenment, the other of fervor; one of knowledge, the other of devotion: so a tender affection, a heart glowing with love, the infusion of holy ardor, and the vigor of a spirit filled

---

61. Leclercq, *Love of Learning and Desire for God*, 73.
62. Toon, *Meditating as a Christian*, 178.
63. Underhill, *Cloud of Unknowing*, 62.
64. Huntley, *Bishop Joseph Hall*, 83.
65. Huntley, *Bishop Joseph Hall*, 59–60.
66. Augustine, "On the Trinity," XII.2.5.168.

with zeal, are obviously not acquired from any place other than the wine-cellar.[67]

Hall could confirm that prayer was the entrance into the wine-cellar of the Spirit's gift of godly inebriation where the sinful self is restrained, not unleashed, so that the reality of spiritual truths come to fruition—"be not drunk with wine, but be filled with the Spirit."[68] "Prayer maketh way for meditation, meditation giveth matter, strength, and life to our prayers."[69] This prayer, according to Hall, should be short—as a portal or door to the experience of meditation, it is but a small step into another room. It is to be a simple asking God to guide, protect, and bless this time of meditation.

The pattern of the main body of *The Art of Meditation*, after the preliminary notes of setting the stage, can be identified as Hall's use of a Ramist style of dialogue. The body of his *Art* is a series of questions to the soul/self and dialogue with God, a dialectic form of writing. For Hall, the essence of meditation was to enter the area of inner dialogue of the soul with God. Hall provided a model of how to dialogue with sample prayers that resemble soulful discourse which addressed the self and then addresses God. It was a dialectic of an interchange that moved and directed the soul upward from thoughts of doubt and sin towards words of confidence and heavenly promise. Speaking to the self and then speaking to God was the double reflexive feature of this engagement—like Jacob at the river Jabbok, it tarried and struggled for a blessing. In Hall, the style of the soliloquy most likely comes from Augustine. It is also found in Anselm, as seen in his *Prosologion*:

> Come now, little man, turn aside for a while from your daily employment, escape for a moment from the tumult of your thoughts. Put aside your weighty cares, let your burdensome distractions wait, free yourself awhile in God and rest awhile in him. Enter the inner chamber of your soul, search out everything but God and that which can help you in seeking him, and when you have shut the door, seek him. Now my whole heart, say to God, "I seek your face, Lord it is your face I seek."[70]

Both the language of Scripture and early Christian authors engaged in this literary style. The Anglican scholar Peter Toon notes, "So addressing oneself to increase determination to succeed is common in human

---

67. Tamburello, *Union with Christ*, 73.
68. Eph 5:18.
69. Huntley, *Bishop Joseph Hall*, 60.
70. Toon, *Meditating as a Christian*, 176.

experience (as sport competitors). The old word for this internal conversation is soliloquy."[71]

> Outside sacred Scriptures, there are many fine examples of the use of soliloquy in the context of meditation and prayer. The great Augustine of Hippo has a book entitled *Soliloquies* and so has Anselm (*Monoloion*). However, the choicest examples of soliloquy that I have read are in the moving book *The Saint's Everlasting Rest* by Richard Baxter, the English Puritan, and in Soliloquies: or holy self-conferences of the devout soul, by Bishop Joseph Hall of Norwich.[72]

The inner dialogue of the soul has a common historiography in the church at large, one that was fully embraced by the Puritans in the practice of contemplation. Understanding the complexity of the soul, they were experts in the internal geography of the soul. Next, Hall outlined the steps of the ladder, while not always clear in his work (the steps are not outlined according to his chapters), they emerged as an upward descent into greater vision and comprehension of divine glory.

Excussion—Choosing the Topic

The entrance also includes choosing the topic of the meditation. Once again, this is not merely picking a topic without much thought, but an inward dialogue of the heart: "inward inquisition made into our heart of what we both do and should think upon, rejecting what is [inexpedient] and unprofitable."[73] The topic is not a matter of outward assignments but a sense of the soul's need and inner longing at the moment. This was true with the English mystics and the practical mindedness in their approach. Chapter 5 will compare and see how Walter Hilton's *Scale of Perfection* and the author of the *Cloud of Unknowing*, both English mystical writers that were part of Hall's source material. Both are written with a sense of being adaptable both in and outside the monastic community. In content and style, they bear much resemblance to Hall's method of meditation. This will be examined in partial texts in this chapter but argued separately as viable source material in chapter 4.

---

71. Toon, *Meditating as a Christian*, 129. Solus = sole; loqui = speak, so this reflects the idea of self-directed speech.

72. Toon, *Meditating as a Christian*, 131.

73. Hall, *Art*, 60.

As the concept of ascent and descent is studied along a literary framework it should be seen that the Huntley diagram of Hall's Ramist structure is one possible construct.[74] There is a correspondence to the steps. Yet, the diagram suggested by Huntley indicates merely an external heuristic key for academic analysis. It was not Hall's intent, as argued here, to offer a literary device, but a practical and spiritual guide. The model is not as structurally designed as might be found in Ignatian approaches, for Hall allowed many variances of approaches and application. The ladder or mountain was a way of describing the actual spiritual direction of this spiritual exercise. As steps counted in total, Hall has eighteen in the actual process of meditation (not including the preparatory stages). Yet the model of Huntley obscures this mental construct, where Hall's method was not to be seen as merely quantitative and linear, but analogically divided into ten steps in the ascent and seven in the descent. This view does not ignore any Ramistic style in Hall's method but affirms an intentional model within the text itself. Hall's method has been at times too obscure and complex for practical use. It becomes clearer to see the structure Hall had in mind to remedy the supposed obscurity of his approach to meditation. This structure fits within an ancient pattern of ascent and descent of monastic spirituality recovered for the needs of Hall's day without the moralistic overtones of other models. Canlis notes the same concern found in Calvin, not often recognized by Reformed scholars: "Humanity's ascent to the Father is not as the moral philosophers envisioned, by 'virtue' and 'nature,' but could only be framed in terms of the Spirit bringing humanity to participate in Christ's ascent . . . Without taking participation in Christ's ascent seriously, the moral philosophers left the human-to-God trajectory to the realm of human response, thus ridding it of koinonia."[75] In the chapters dealing with Hall's use of patristic sources, it will be seen that Hall was deeply indebted to Augustinian monastic traditions and to Eastern fathers. Like Calvin, Hall drew from a broad range of the Christian tradition, and the environment of seventeenth-century London availed him of a rich repository of texts and scholars who were familiar with this breadth of scholarship. Referring to Calvin's use of these sources of early church antiquity, Colin Gunton states, "despite his heavy dependence upon Augustine, [Hall] was also a careful reader of Eastern, including the

---

74. Hall, *Art*, 21–23. Opposing truths or dialectics are placed in a practice of piety or dialogue of the soul, aimed not at academic polemics but inner dialogue of the soul. Huntley adds, "One must not overlook his two examples, which are a final and overwhelming dichotomy: 'The one of eternal life, as the end. The other is Death, as the way'" (Huntley, *Bishop Joseph Hall*, 12).

75. Canlis, *Calvin's Ladder*, 128.

Cappadocian Fathers..."[76] Out of this reading of the Reformed appreciation of Eastern Fathers, it is reasonable to see where Hall would find appreciation for contemplative practices outside the oversight of Tridentine Rome.

In the Eastern tradition stands the well-known monk from Mount Sinai John Climacus (579–649), also known as "John Scholasticus," from his fourteen-hundred-year-old classic *The Ladder of Divine Assent*. John's thirty steps in the ladder are meant to guide those in the pursuit of the ascetical life into deeper reflection of the divine life and vision of Christ. From the foot of Mount Sinai at St. Catherine's monastery, John was asked to present a helpful instructional aid for monks and laity. It is very possible, given its wide reception, that Hall had knowledge of this Eastern work. Hence, having eighteen steps compared to this earlier tradition of thirty revealed a further simplification and adaptation for Hall's contemporary audience.[77]

The problem of sources will be addressed in chapter 4, but here it is enough to state that while Hall did not name all his sources, it will be argued that a wide range of material both Western and Eastern provided a rich background of a spirituality of ascent for meditation and contemplative prayer. There were political and theological reasons for this, as the English Protestant church sought to claim its apostolic legitimacy away from Rome. Given this historical context, it must be highlighted that Joseph Hall was motivated to bring a spiritual practice that would actually improve the lives of his fellow countrymen in forming their souls towards genuine and affectious love of God. In this vein, Hall's *Art* provided ten steps in preparing the understanding for proper contemplation.

SECOND PART: PROCEEDING OF THE MEDITATION

Hall's method was divided into two sections; the first steps dealt with the mind and understanding. Its ten steps were to prepare the soul through a cognitive and deliberate thinking over the topic. "Ere I enter, therefore, into any particular tractation, there are three things whereof I would premonish my reader concerning this first part, which is the understanding."[78]

Hall stated that he has found a helpful scale—an outline of the ascent for meditation—a type of ladder found in ancient divines (he names Origen,

---

76. Gunton, *Father, Son, and Holy Spirit*, 41, 51. This supports the view of how Reformed orthodoxy valued the thinking of the Eastern Church in regard to the Trinity.

77. Climacus, *Ladder of Divine Ascent*, 1. The popularity of *The Ladder* in the East equals that of *The Imitation of Christ* in the West, although the two books are altogether different in character.

78. Huntley, *Bishop Joseph Hall*, 88.

Austin, Bernard, Bonaventure, and Gerson). The scale was borrowed from Mauburnus's work *The Rosetum*, published in 1494.[79] But, as asserted previously, Hall's steps or ladder was not a hard-and-fast rule, and even Hall acknowledged that if this scale proves to be difficult or obtuse, it was better to move on to other steps than to "strive more for logic than devotion."[80] The rungs of the ladder were not to be seen as indispensable steps legalistically imposed for the devout seeker. Breaking one's teeth over the shell, as Hall stated, would leave little enjoyment of the kernel.[81] Harkening the same concern as the English mystic, "And therefore let us pick off the rough bark, and feed us off the sweet kernel."[82] Hence, the "kernel" of sweet devotion was the concern, as Hall moved the reader through this model of meditation he wisely advised that the practitioner need not be bound "exactly to the rules of art."[83] He allowed for variance and suggestions that appear to be offered but not demanded as necessities. "First, I desire not to bind every man to the same uniform proceeding in this part. Practice and custom may perhaps have taught other courses more familiar and not less direct."[84] Breaking the topic of meditation into divisions, according to Hall, should come in a "voluntary" and natural way. Speaking to the soul, the spiritual pilgrim should remind the soul that it was created to dwell in a body and that divine grace offered by the Holy Spirit renews the soul. "When the body being united to thee (soul), both shall be united to God."[85] It was a dialogue, with the soul reminding herself of her journey, filled with the natural stages of life until death, but will one day behold glory and the splendor of eternity. This was language that prepared the soul for heavenly communion in stabs of joy on this side of glory. Hall's suggested topic for the model of meditation was heaven or the future glory of the saint. His conclusion included a chapter on death, whereby he showed a shorter model about human mortality. Thus, two examples are given by Hall to provide a type of template that can be adapted for any use.

79. Huntley, *Bishop Joseph Hall*, 61.
80. Huntley, *Bishop Joseph Hall*, 89.
81. Huntley, *Bishop Joseph Hall*, 62.
82. Underhill, *Cloud of Unknowing*, 101.
83. Huntley, *Bishop Joseph Hall*, 88.
84. Huntley, *Bishop Joseph Hall*, 88.
85. Huntley, *Bishop Joseph Hall*, 88.

Step One to Step Four

Reflecting on the topic of heaven, Hall invited the pilgrim to a dialogue with the soul.

> What, then, O my soul, is the life of the saints whereof thou studiest? Who are the saints but those which, having been weakly holy upon earth, are perfectly holy above; which even on earth were perfectly holy in their Saviour, now are so in themselves; which, overcoming on earth, are truly canonized in heaven?[86]

It is central to the Protestant view of sanctification that the spiritual life is not exclusive to a specialized few but a calling for all Christians. Sainthood is the path of every redeemed soul that longs and indeed seeks its true native homeland beyond the confines of this earthly coil, the body. Walter Hilton in a similar way instructed his reader:

> This way of knowing Jesus, as I understand, is the opening of heaven to the eye of a pure soul, of which holy men speak in their writings. Not as some suppose, that the opening of heaven is as if a soul could see by imagination through the skies above the firmament, how our Lord Jesus sits in his majesty in a bodily light as great as a hundred suns.[87]

Both *The Cloud of Unknowing* and *The Scale of Perfection* appear to be part of Hall's background in thinking about the glory of heaven, which was not fanciful travel but possessing fullness of joy in Jesus.

Step two in Hall's model was making a distinction in addressing the unique quality of the soul in this type of contemplation. Hall called this a "voluntary" division. Addressing the soul, the question was directed towards its true end: "There is a life of nature when thou, my soul, dwellest in this body and informest thine earthly burthen. There was a life of grace when the spirit of God dwells in thee. There is a life of glory when thy body meantime being separated from thy companion, thou enjoyest God alone."[88]

Life has stages, and so does the soul in its journey. Human life on the stage of the world is lived out in seasons. Yet, in a spiritual sense, the soul that is the inner person also has a process of development and growth towards immortal life. Hall reflected this idea in referring to the soul:

> This life of thine (soul), therefore, as the other, hath his ages, hath his statures; for it entereth upon his birth when thou passeth out

---

86. Huntley, *Bishop Joseph Hall*, 89.
87. Hilton, *Scale of Perfection*, 261.
88. Huntley, *Bishop Joseph Hall*, 90.

of thy body and changest this earthly house for an heavenly. It enters into his full vigor when, at the day of the common resurrection, thou resumest this thy companion, unlike to itself, like to thee, like to thy Saviour, immortal now and glorious.[89]

In the third step, Hall is referring to reflecting on the source of this heavenly gift. He is reminding the soul to take the knowledge of its blessings towards an affective experiential love of its primary source. The causality of divine blessedness is in God alone, it is not rooted or initiated on the part of the soul. The soul is responsive to divine grace that elects and calls by God's love to the "Author of life."

> The Father bestoweth it, the Son meriteth it, the Holy Ghost seals and applieth it. Expect it only from Him, O my soul, whose free election gave thee thy first title to it, to be purchased by the blood of thy Saviour. For thou shalt not therefore be happy because He said that Thou wouldst be good, but therefore are thou good because He hath ordained thou shalt be happy.[90]

In urging the soul to look unto the Author of life, Hall captured the language of desire and of nuptial longing to be "ravished" with divine love. Its Bernardian tone reflected a language of the soul that the Puritan imagination fully embraced and used prolifically in their spiritual devotions. Marital love and communion between Christ and the church was the basis of directing affective longings for spiritual blessing.

> What is there in this not His? And yet not His so simply as that it is without thee; without thy merit indeed, not without thine act. Thou livest here through His blessing but by bread; though shalt live above through His mercy but by thy faith below apprehending the Author of thy life. And yet, as He will not save thee without thy faith, so thou canst never have faith without His gift. Look up to Him, therefore, O my soul, as the beginner and finisher of thy salvation; and while thou magnifies the Author, be ravished with the glory of the work, which far passeth both the tongues of angels and the heart of man.[91]

Hall noted the power of this longing in the soul, and it is found in other great and ancient spiritual masters. In the *Ladder of Divine Ascent*, John Climacus writes, "Prayer, after all, is a turning away from the world, visible and invisible. What have I in heaven? Nothing. What have I longed

---

89. Huntley, *Bishop Joseph Hall*, 90.
90. Huntley, *Bishop Joseph Hall*, 91.
91. Huntley, *Bishop Joseph Hall*, 91.

for on earth besides You? Nothing except simply to cling always to You in undistracted prayer . . . Faith gives wings to prayer, and without it no one can fly upward to heaven."[92]

The fifth step was *considering* the wonderful mystery of being "ravished with God's glory." Hall had the soul consider the effect of this experience of joy to turn it towards the fruit of happiness, or the fount of true joy. This step was one of great encouragement to a soul catching a future vision of divine glory that erupted in beautiful music of the heavenly courts.

> No marvel, then if from this glory proceed unspeakable joy, and from this joy the sweet songs of praise and thanksgiving. The Spirit bids us when we are merry, sing. How much more, then, when we are merry without mixture of sorrow, beyond all measure of our earthly affections, shall we sing joyful "Hallelujahs" and "Hosannahs" to Him that dwelleth in the highest heavens [Matt 21:9]! Our hearts shall be so full that we cannot choose but to sing, and we cannot but sing melodiously. There is no jar in this music, no end of this song. O blessed charge of the saints![93]

Meditation that erupted in singing to God was not unknown nor seen as extraordinary. Since the Creator gave us bodies, minds, hearts, and voices, the whole person is engaged and enlisted in this divine art. Music is another theme found in mystical texts that the Puritans utilized unreservedly, and Hall both in his intentional and occasional meditations reflected often on music and its role in expressing beauty and the inner language of the soul. In the successive inner chambers of Israel's temple, adoration of God moves inward and towards closer, even if restrictive, entrance to divine glory.

Steps Six to Ten

Step six is the subject of our future glory and home, filled with nuptial imagery of the soul finding its bridegroom in a union of full delight.

> And, indeed, what less happiness doth the very place promise wherein this glory is exhibited, which is no other than the paradise of God? Here below we dwell, or rather wander in a continued wilderness; there we shall rest us in the true Eden. "I am come into my garden, my Sister, my Spouse" [Cant 4:12]. Kings use not to dwell in cottages of clay but in royal courts fit

---

92. Climacus, *Ladder of Divine Ascent*, 277.
93. Huntley, *Bishop Joseph Hall*, 92.

for their estate. How much more shall the King of Heaven, who hath prepared so fair mansions on earth, make Himself a habitation suitable to His majesty![94]

Like John Climacus's *Ladder of Ascent*, Hall noted the bridal imagery of dwelling in the chamber next to the King. "O my brothers, we should run to enter the bridal chamber of this palace, and if some burden of past habits or the passage of time should impede us, what a disaster for us! Let us at least take up residence in one of the mansions near the bridal chamber."[95]

In the next step (attention), the soul continued the dialogue with itself upon this inner longing. This practice was also an ancient and biblical practice seen from the Psalms of David to the prayers of Augustine. "The soliloquy, a meditative style handed down from Augustine, entailed "a pleading the case with thyself."[96] The soul was meant for more than this world; there is a call for another country, a longing for a reality that is its true home. "There shalt thou live familiarly in the sight of those angels whom now thou receives good from, but seest not."[97] J. I. Packer writes this concerning the Puritan vision of heaven: "Sanctified imagination gives concreteness and colour to theological perception, resulting in extraordinary power to convey the flow of glory to the Christian heart."[98] At this stage in meditation the soul was enticed to long and desire heaven not for its place but for its inhabitant. "I sought him whom my soul loveth; I sought him but found him not." Hall then added a note of the experience of absence, as though full union is not possible: "His back is now towards thee many times through thy sins . . . thou hardly discernest him. Otherwhile, and often, thy back is turned unto him through negligence." The reality of sinful distance and earthly dissonance was experienced in heavenly ecstasy reflective of the temporal nature of this hint of glory that was still transcendent to human experience.

> Now thou shalt see him, and thine eyes, thus fixed, shall not be removed. Yet neither could this glory make us happy if, being

---

94. Huntley, *Bishop Joseph Hall*, 92–93.
95. Climacus, *Ladder of Divine Ascent*, 284.
96. Senn, *Protestant Spiritual Traditions*, 174.
97 Huntley, *Bishop Joseph Hall*, 93.
98. Packer, *A Quest for Godliness*, 334. Packer is referencing the authors that followed Hall in the use of meditation and the imagination, namely Richard Baxter and John Bunyan and the way they envisioned the glory of heaven in their examples with its desire and longing captured in beautiful images. "Beatification" is not a term used by the Puritans and is usually associated with Eastern Orthodoxy theology, but it fits the criteria of how both traditions saw the spiritual experience as attainable. See a comprehensive study of this doctrine as it relates to both traditions especially written for Protestant readership in the recent work of Hans Boersma, *Seeing God*.

> thus absolute, it were not perpetual. To be happy is not so sweet a state as it is miserable to have been happy. Lest ought, therefore, should be wanting, behold, this felicity knoweth no end, feareth no intermission, and is as eternal for the continuance as He that had no beginning.[99]

Here in this step Hall saw the pilgrim moving toward contemplation of pure joy and timelessness in the face of the Beloved. It was the beatification and vision of one's union with Christ, not in its final consummation but in a grace-filled glimpse, like the three disciples experienced on the Mount of Transfiguration. It was not an ascent to be united to Christ (soteriological), but the ascent to the joy and fruit (sanctification by the Spirit) of union with Christ that made the ascent possible and desirable. The experience of this infinite joy and beauty was, however, a fleeting one, not ever fully realized or possessed by the saint. Using language that described this regress of a pilgrim's attainment, Hall imagined, as argued here, the climb down the mountain as part of the meditation. Two visions are glanced: as it saw both the glory that was promised, the inward eyes also see the mortal restrictions of the present life.

The seventh step was referred to as a descent—a stepping back where the soul considered the *comparison* or opposite of this divine fellowship. Using very practical and real-life struggles and discomforts, the body, it seems, reminds the soul that through aches, pains, physical needs, and worldly concerns it will not allow the soul to stay in bliss.[100] The question may arise that if this is a ladder of ascent, why is there a regression on this step? With skillful wisdom, Hall's understanding of the pathology of the soul affirmed the struggle that people have in spiritual formation. Like Bunyan's traveling pilgrim, the road towards the celestial city was not a straight line, but a road of turns and setbacks. The soul was replete with longings that cloud and confuse the desire for God. Even within the soul the struggle with sin was ongoing: "Thou needest not fetch cause of complaint from others; thy corruptions yield thee too much at home: ever sinning, ever presuming, sinning even when though hast repented, yea, even while thou repentest, sinning."[101]

Meditation is not free from this familiar dilemma. Then there is the dual tension of the anticipation of glory and the realization of the absence of God's presence. Both realities are worthy of the soul's pondering. As the poet Dante expressed through Beatrice, the journey towards heaven must reflect on the despair of eternal damnation. Ola E. Winslow's account of

---

99. Huntley, *Bishop Joseph Hall*, 94.
100. Huntley, *Bishop Joseph Hall*, 67.
101. Huntley, *Bishop Joseph Hall*, 95.

Edward's preaching is reflective of this notion: "Could Dante do more? In fact, one contemplates Dante's hell with pleasurable sensations, knowing it is Dante's, a safely remote place of the imagination. Jonathan Edwards not only made it real enough to be found in the atlas, but made those consigned to it personally responsible for being there."[102] The misunderstanding that exists by those who are only slightly familiar with Jonathan Edwards's famous sermon *Sinners in the Hands of an Angry God* believe that the Puritan imagination is conditioned more by fear and psychological deficiencies and fail to appreciate the complexity of the soul's longing for true glory and joy in divine mercy.

Speaking to the soul as a reminder of the strangeness of this bodily existence, the soul is asked to ponder the agonies of hell. This Dionysian dialectic moves from a contemplation on our future condition apart from divine mercy and puts divine justice in the context of the glory to come. The pains and aches of hell are of no comparison to the sufferings of this present life; this provides perspective and enlarges the heart for greater love and appreciation for divine grace and mercy. To those like Edwards's adversary, Rev. Charles Chauncy, who viewed such an approach as mere enthusiasm and even manipulative, the assumption of these theological truths of damnation and glory are on the side of this historical thread of contemplative piety. Hall, much like Edwards who followed him, combined reason with passion for a spirituality engaged in imagination reflecting on true spiritual realities.

Throughout this model, Hall used many allusions to the Song of Solomon. Historian Frank Senn affirms this relationship: "Like the medieval contemplatives such as Bernard of Clairvaux, the Puritans relied on the Song of Songs as well as New Testament passages such as the passion narratives."[103] In like manner to Bernard and a Kempis, the soul of the believer as well as the church is the feminine actor as the besought bride who is both hidden and longs for the elusive lover of her soul. Theologically it reflects two poles of the Christian experience of grace. Arie de Reuver, in reflecting on Bernard's application of these texts, indicates this stress: "However involved the soul of the bride is in these intimate events, their occurrence is not the result of cooperation but of unilateral grace. In them the souls are not productive, but receptive. It is also fully aware of this fact. Bernard regards this gracious encounter as impossible, then, without humble self-knowledge."[104] It signi-

---

102. Winslow, *Jonathan Edwards*, 193.
103. Senn, *Protestant Spiritual Traditions*, 174.
104. Reuver, *Sweet Communion*, 54.

fied the *mystica union* that is a gift of imputed grace of justification, but it also sustains a rich, unfulfilled, and ongoing work of the Spirit.

The nuptial relationship of the soul to Christ was the key analogy for this spiritual union. As the soul moved from a dialectic of pondering the dangers of damnation as the end of those who love sin and wicked desires, Hall had the soul consider the taste of glory in step eight. As when the disciples saw Jesus on Mt. Tabor, they desired to stay and build a tent, the soul's taste of God's goodness was a foretaste of the coming wedding feast.

> But the marriage-feast of the Son of God to His blessed Spouse the Church must so far exceed in all heavenly magnificence and variety as the persons are of the greater state and majesty. There is new wine, pure manna, and all manner of spiritual dainties; and with the continual cheer a sweet and answerable welcome, while the Bridegroom lovingly cheerth us up: "Eat, O my friends, drink and make you merry. O well beloved" [Cant 5:1]. Yea, there shalt thou be, my soul, not a guest but (how unworthy soever) the bride herself whom He hath everlastingly espoused to Himself in truth and righteousness . . . "My well-beloved is mine, and I am his: where fore hearken," O my soul, and consider, and incline thine ear; forget also thine own people, and thy father's house, thy supposed home of this world; so shall the King have pleasure in thy beauty; for he is the Lord, and worship thou him.[105]

The soul is comforted with the possessive knowledge that she is not merely a guest to the wedding, she is the bride. Ascending further up this mount, the pilgrim is filled with greater longing, and Hall reminds her to forget "thy father's house" and look for the greater joy ahead. In one of Hall's occasional meditations, reflecting on seeing a wedding, he wrote,

> Oh gracious Saviour, as Thou canst not but love and cherish this poor and unworthy soul of mine, which Thou hast mercifully espoused to Thyself, so give me grace to honor and obey Thee and, forsaking all the base and sinful rivality of the world, to hold me only unto Thee while I live here, that I may perfectly enjoy Thee hereafter.[106]

Then with psychological reflection on the soul's temporal condition, the ninth step was the discernment or classification of this experience of the soul. The soul was reminded of this pilgrimage that points beyond itself to a lasting reality. "What is more dear to us than our country? Which the

---

105. Huntley, *Bishop Joseph Hall*, 70.
106. Hall, *Occasional Meditation*, "Upon the Sight of a Marriage," 162.

worthy and faithful patriots of all times have respected above their parents, their children, their lives?"[107] There was a hint of homesickness that has a positive purpose to lure the troubled soul from lethargy and despair. "Where is our country, but above? O what affections can be worthy of such a home!"[108] Hall's image of the pilgrim, a traveler to another country, was combined with the nuptial imagery of the Song of Solomon throughout this meditation. The interior country of the soul was recast as a weary journey that ended with unexpected joy and delight which provided a soul so prone to languish in melancholy and sinful despondency to long for its true glorified state. One can see Bunyan's pilgrim with the similar dialectic of moving back and forth in his journey to the Celestial City. After being richly fed and nourished from the Lord of the Hill, Christian faced a fierce battle in the Valley of Humiliation. "Now at the end of this valley was another . . . and Christian must needs go through it, because the way to the *Celestial City* lies through the midst of it: now this valley is a very solitary place."[109] Hall affirmed that the dialectic of longing and suffering was indicative of a realization that the true home is a future destination.

Hall's tenth step was to consider the confirmation of Scripture related to the topic. Here we see Hall's application of *sola scriptura*, "none but divine authority can command assent and settle the conscience"—the final authority of the word in matters related to meditation. [110]"Witnesses of holy men may serve for colours, but the ground must be only from God."[111] Ancient guides of the saints are good markers, but surety is found in the word of God. The hope of a lasting and glorious home for the pilgrim is not rooted in fantasy or wish fulfillment, but on the promises of Scripture.[112]

Step Eleven: The Mount of Vision

The second part of meditation (if one is not lost on the parts and the steps) was the focus on the affections—to taste and relish what has been pondered, according to Hall. If this step is viewed as the summit, as this study suggests, then the culmination of the understanding and use of the mind on meditation is moved to the affective aspect of the soul. But this is not to be seen as

107. Huntley, *Bishop Joseph Hall*, 71.
108. Huntley, *Bishop Joseph Hall*, 71.
109. Bunyan, *Pilgrim's Progress*, 65.
110. Huntley, *Bishop Joseph Hall*, 99.
111. Huntley, *Bishop Joseph Hall*, 71.
112. Huntley, *Bishop Joseph Hall*, 72.

a sequential transition, but is often a cyclical movement, more as a dance rather than a marathon.

Going from the difficult part of meditation, Hall moved the reader (chapter 28) to that which is more delightful, "which is both more lively and more easy unto a good heart."[113] Here one finds "the very soul of meditation."[114] This showed how the affections are the key element of the soul's experience in this holy ascent in "beholding" the glory of the Savior. Moving beyond an exercise of the mind, the affections are marshaled for godly pursuits in inflaming the will towards a native habitat, the abiding presence of God in the soul. Frank Senn notes, "And Puritans could report experiences worthy of a Bernard of Clairvaux or a Teresa of Avila. Cotton Mather, for instance, spoke of his heart being 'rapt into those heavenly Frames, which would have turned a Dungeon into a Paradise' or 'raised unto Raptures almost Insupportable, when I was Expressing my Love to God, and Believing His Love to me . . .'"[115] The experience of rapture and spiritual vision of Jesus was something that moved beyond rational explanation. Indeed, it is the essence of mystical union. Hall noted the primacy of the volitional aspect of faith as leading towards an experiential reality of knowing God. "A man is a man by his understanding part, but he is a Christian by his will and affection."[116] This resonates with the view of Calvin, who wrote, "Faith consists in the knowledge of Christ; Christ cannot be known without the sanctification of his Spirit: therefore, faith cannot possibly be disjoined from pious affection."[117]

The priority of the will in faith is the connecting theme that runs through Hall, Gerson, Bonaventure, and even, arguably, Calvin, even though many consider him to have an intellectualist view of faith. Calvin's definition of faith was a "firm and sure knowledge of the divine favor toward us, founded on the truth of a free promise in Christ, and revealed to our minds, and sealed on our hearts, by the Holy Spirit."[118] But this definition of faith as a "sure knowledge" is not without the affections verifying it as authentic faith. Again, Calvin asserts, "faith cannot possibly be disjoined from pious affection."[119] The role of the will and its relationship to reason is conveyed

---

113. Huntley, *Bishop Joseph Hall*, 100.

114. Hall, *Art of Meditation*, 72. This is in chapter 28; as a note to readers, the chapters are not paginated with the steps, so the chapter numbers do not correspond to the steps. This can be difficult to follow.

115. Senn, *Protestant Spiritual Traditions*, 171.

116. Huntley, *Bishop Joseph Hall*, 100.

117. Calvin, *Institutes* III.2.8.

118. Calvin, *Institutes* III.2.7.

119. Calvin, *Institutes* III.2.8.

by Hall in saying, "our former labour of the brain is only to affect the heart, after that the mind hath thus traversed the point proposed through all the heads of reason, it shall endeavor to find, in the first place, some feeling touch and sweet relish in that which it hath thus chewed." The will does not dominate reason, and neither does reason need to be overcome by will, for they work together to create a desire that reveals that reason by itself, understanding without affection, is void of true faith.

> David saith, O taste and see how sweet the Lord is. In meditation we do both see and taste; but we see before we taste; sight is of the understanding; taste, of the affection; neither can we see, but we must taste; we cannot know right, but we must needs be affected. Let the heart, therefore, first conceive and feel itself the sweetness or bitterness of the matter meditated, which is never done without some passion, nor expressed without some hearty exclamation: "Oh blessed estate of the saints! Oh glory not to be expressed even by those who are glorified! Oh incomprehensible salvation! What favor hat this earth to thee? Who can regard the world that believeth thee? Who can think of thee and not be ravished with wonder and desire? Who can think of thee and not be ravished with wonder and desire?"[120]

According to the Bible, faith is "not seen" with physical eyes, but it is seeing with inward eyes that have been enlightened by redemptive grace in the soul.[121] The argument to be made is not a strict voluntarist view of faith that prioritizes the will apart from the faculty of understanding but places the two in a dialectic of movement so that they belong together. Yet, the emphasis on the will in being commandeered or enlivened by the affections is not undermined but upheld. To put it simply, longing precedes understanding.

As Hall reminds the reader, "Let the heart, therefore, first conceive and feel in itself the sweetness or bitterness of the matter meditated; which is never done without some passion."[122] There is a temporal order of understanding and reasoning that leads to the affections, but the soul is a complex reality that experiences and moves beyond the lines of the rational faculty of the mind. Chapter 5 will probe these issues more deeply as the theology of the soul and its faculties is studied and related to the work of Hall and later

---

120. Huntley, *Bishop Joseph Hall*, 72.

121. Eph 1:18: "The eyes of your understanding being enlightened; that ye may know what is the hope of his calling, and what the riches of the glory of his inheritance in the saints."

122. Huntley, *Bishop Joseph Hall*, 100–101.

Puritans. A more recent theologian from the Dutch tradition aptly points to this important issue as it relates to a broad spectrum of thinking about human nature. Herman Bavinck wrote:

> The proper starting point for any theory of knowledge is the universal and natural certainty we find spontaneously in our ordinary experience. We trust our senses, which lead us to believe in an objective world external to us, and our mental representations of that world point back to that reality. From this we conclude that scientific demonstrative certainty is neither the basic nor the only kind of human certainty; there is also a universal, metaphysical, intuitive, immediate kind of certainty that is self-evident and which we call the "certainty of faith."[123]

Steps of Descent: An Inward and Downward Journey

Moving with the dialectic of bliss and joy back to earthborne misery, the reader expresses complaint that the soul is yet so poor and forlorn in spite of this taste of joy. "But alas! Where is my love? Where is my longing? Where are thou, O my soul? . . . moving from promise to doubt the soul cries, 'Dost thou doubt whether there be an heaven? Or whether thou have a God and a Savior there? O far be from thee this atheism.'"[124] As unexpectantly did the joy appear it was gone, so that the loss seemed ever the sharper and empty than before. There is resolution for the doubter not in reason but in the desire. It does not diminish the desire to have the taste of divine joy, but it revealed that the human longing is always incomplete. Hall described this experience in a complaint towards the soul's lack of desire. "But, O thou of little faith, dost thou believe there is happiness, and happiness for thee; and desirest it not, and delightest not in it? . . . how cold and faint are thy desires!"[125] This desire for God as a capacity for longing and experiencing the knowledge of God was rooted in St. Bonaventure.[126]

---

123. Bavinck, *Reformed Dogmatics*, 1:208. He continues to state, "Christian thinkers from Augustine on rejected rationalism in favor of a 'realism' that acknowledges the primacy of the senses and the constraints placed by reality on the human mind. At the same time, in distinction from empiricist thought, Christian theology also insists that the mind does have its own nature, operates in its own way, and possesses the freedom to soar beyond the senses to the world of the ideal . . . The theological explanation for this is the conviction that the same Logos created both the reality outside of us and the laws of thought within us."

124. Huntley, *Bishop Joseph Hall*, 91.

125. Huntley, *Bishop Joseph Hall*, 73.

126. Copleston, *Medieval Philosophy*, 77.

THE ART OF MEDITATION: ANALYSIS

In the third step of descent, as this study describes this inward journey, the soul was to ponder this inner longing and holy desire for God. Hall captured it well in this passage:

> O that my heart could be rapt up thither in desire! How should I trample upon these poor vanities of the earth! How willingly should I endure all sorrows, all torments! How scornfully should I pass by all pleasures! How should I be in travail of my dissolution! Oh when shall that blessed day come when, all this wretched worldliness removed, I shall solace myself in God?[127]

He ends quoting the Psalms, "As a hart pants . . ." (Psalm 42), capturing the psalmist's imagery of desire that comes from deep in the soul for God. This was the desire that comes from an insatiable longing affected by "a glimpse of heaven." The descent was the realization of longing and hope that was delayed, not fully realized even in the apex of tasting the glory. Like the veiling of Moses, it was a glory that faded, for permanence is a quality of another world.

The next step is part confessional, but only in the sense of realizing human limitations. Looking now inward, not by confession of sin, so much as a confession of human inability to fulfill this longing and ache of the heart. This type of acknowledgment moved beyond the first stage of purgation, to a confession of human incapacity in a world of sin to continue on the summit of holy contemplation. This was a movement downward, not to a place of judgment, but a realization of sorrow over the delay. It is the cry of the church: "Come quickly, Lord Jesus." (Rev 22:20).

> Being lifted up with our estate of joy, it is cast down with complaint; fit up with wishes, it is cast down with confession, which order doth best hot in ure and just temper and maketh it more feeling of the comfort which followeth in the conclusion. This confession must derogate all from ourselves and ascribe all to God: "I desire to come to Thee, but alas, how weakly, how heartlessly! Thou nowest that I can neither come to Thee nor desire to come but from Thee. It is nature that holds me from Thee; this treacherous nature favors itself, loveth the world, hateth to thin of a dissolution, and chooseth rather to dwell in this dungeon with continual sorrow and complaint that to endure a parting although to liberty and joy . . . Thou only . . . canst fix my soul upon heaven and Thee.[128]

---

127. Huntley, *Bishop Joseph Hall*, 102.
128. Hall, *Art*, 103.

The pilgrim on descent petitioned God for the scales of blindness to be removed. Hall recognized the experience of beatific vision was not just a future reality, but an inward experience of grace. Redemption is more than the hope of getting to heaven; it is the hope of getting heaven into the soul. "Oh Thou that hast prepared a place for my soul [John 14:2], prepare my soul for that place; prepare it with holiness; prepare it with desire; and even while it sojourneth on earth let it dwell in heaven with Thee, beholding ever the beauty of Thy face."[129] Coming after Hall and influenced by him, Thomas Watson's book on meditation states, "Meditation sweetly puts us in heaven before we arrive there. Meditation brings God and the soul together."[130] This fifth step was a petition or a cry to God for the grace to be better equipped for heaven while upon this earthly journey.

Ever concerned about the danger of empty words and mindless routine, step six recalled the need to reflect deeply upon the prior petition in prayer. Hence, it looked into the heart to bring fire and feeling to the request. A prayer made with a cold heart falls like a dead weight from the lips of vanity. As meditation is aimed more at the affections, this step lingered on the theme of right affections. While much of the prior steps in the ascent were soliloquies of the soul to itself, steps five and six are ardent prayers to God. The dialogue is of a soul's inability to attain what it desires.

> O let me see heaven another while and love it so much more than the earth by how much the things there are more worthy to be loved. Oh God, look down on Thy wretched pilgrim and teach me to look up to Thee and to see Thy goodness in the land of the living. Thou that boughtest heaven for me, guide me thither, and for the price it cost Thee, for Thy mercy's sake in spite of all temptations, enlighten my soul, direct it, crown it.[131]

One Lutheran author recognizes the element of commonality between ancient medieval practice and English Protestants: "Early on, Puritans perfected methods of meditation and contemplation supportive of heart religion. This is seen in Richard Baxter's work on role of meditation in prayer, 'affections are key to true heart faith.'"[132] This connecting theme in Baxter will be considered in chapter 4, the next step completes the journey that Hall has emulated from other ancient sources.

This final and seventh step of descent ended with bringing a bold assurance to the soul, that its petitions can be safeguarded upon the promises

---

129. Hall, *Art*, 203.
130. Watson, *Christian on the Mount*, 92.
131. Hall, *Art*, 105.
132. Senn, *Protestant Spiritual Traditions*, 172.

of God. Confidence is rooted in divine trustworthiness of our surety in God's covenantal and unilateral grace to the undeserving. It was a cry of assurance to the truth that the reality of glory is to be fully trusted. This step was not a final end to meditation, for as Hall made clear, the process can go on depending on the need and desire of the soul. Rumination is an ongoing experience of taking the meditation further into one's experience for meditation to be lived and applied throughout the day.

CONCLUSION OF MEDITATION: THANKSGIVING, RECOMMENDATION, EXHORTATION

The idea of rumination is "to think deeply" or a "chewing the cud" which is a repeating of the stairs of the meditation until affections are stirred and is a recurring theme in medieval meditation. Using the language of descent in the final stages of this art, Hall advised a slow entrance "by degrees back to a life of active obedience ending in a prayer of thanksgiving to God. Does Hall expect this process to have affected the heart? Is he concerned with the value and the role of the affections in shaping the right order of the soul? It would be difficult to deny this in his concluding remarks:

> This course of meditation thus heartily observed, let him that practiceth it tell me whether he find not that his soul, which at the beginning of this exercise did but creep and grovel upon earth, do not now in the conclusion soar aloft in heaven and, being before aloof off, do not now find itself near to God, yea, with Him and in Him.[133]

This abandonment to divine grace was reflected in the latter part of Book Two in Hilton's *Scale of Perfection*: "For since the soul sees that its own love is nothing, it therefore wants his love, for that is enough; for that he prays and that he desires: that the love of God would touch him with its blessed light, so that he could see a little of him by his gracious presence; for then he should love him; and so by this way the gift of love that is God comes into a soul."[134]

In his epilogue, Hall affirmed the great value that meditation has for the soul and encouraged others to use any other model or if they have none of their own, to use his. He ended with these words of warning on this Christian duty:

---

133. Huntley, *Bishop Joseph Hall*, 107.
134. Hilton, *Scale of Perfection*, 267.

> This is the very end God had given us our souls for; we misspend them if we use them not thus. How lamentable is it that we so employ them as if our faculty of discourse served for nothing but our earthly provision, as if our reasonable and Christian minds were appointed for the slaves and drudges of this body, only to be the caters and cooks of our appetite![135]

Our desires are given to us by God not for the base use towards selfish and sinful ends but to refit them by the renewing work of the Spirit for holy ends. As Hall explained in the beginning of his book, "One saith (and I believe him)[136] that God's school is more of affection than understanding... And he that hath much skill and no affection may do good to others by information of judgment, but shall never have thanked either of his own heart or of God, who useth not to cast away His love on those of whom He is but known, not loved."[137] The emphasis on the affections and the use of meditation to rise above natural reasoning is found in Dionysius, Basil, Augustine, John Climacus, Bernard, a Kempis, *The Cloud of Unknowing*, and Hilton.

In a similar vein, Hilton ends his work with saying,

> The voice of our Lord Jesus making ready the harts, and he shall show the thickets. That is, the inspiration of Jesus makes souls as lights as the harts that leap from the earth over the bushes and briars of all worldly vanity, and he shows them the thickets, which are his secrets: they cannot be perceived except by a sharp eye. Truly grounded in grace and humility, these contemplations make a soul wise, burning in desire for the face of Jesus.[138]

Hall reflected this rich history of thinking and therefore is neither an innovator of mysticism in danger of quietism or enthusiasm but a careful interpreter of a biblical and Christological piety long embedded in the tradition of orthodoxy. The next chapter will develop the threads of the historical sources Hall had available in his time.

The Art of Meditation ended with an example of these steps of contemplation applied to the topic of death as an example to follow in using this method. This gave the reader the ability to see how the method was to actually work on a given subject not for moralistic ends but for a greater love for Christ. This was not a Pelagian method of improving the soul nor

---

135. Huntley, *Bishop Joseph Hall*, 107–08.

136. See Connolly, *John Gerson: Reformer and Mystic*, 292. This is very close to a statement by Gerson and is another example of the esteem that Hall had for Gerson.

137. Huntley, *Bishop Joseph Hall*, 72.

138. Hilton, *Scale of Perfection*, 302.

a scholastic framework of complex intricacies with a labyrinth of turns in speculation. The example of Hall reflected this Christological emphasis in moving towards the face of Jesus with the aid of Christ's mercy and in imitation of his humility. John Climacus, ending his *Scale* with a summary and exhortation, clearly delineates his guide for pilgrims not in a structure of moralistic infusion of virtues, even though virtues are addressed, but a recasting the soul in the image of divine love.

> Ascend my brothers, ascend eagerly. Let your hearts' resolve be to climb. Listen to the voice of the one who says: "Come, let us go up to the mountain of the Lord, to the house of our God" (Isa 2:3), Who makes our feet to be like the feet of the deer, "Who sets us on the high places, that we may be triumphant on His road" (Hab 3:19). Run, I beg you, run with him who said, "Let us hurry until we arrive at the unity of faith and the knowledge of God, at mature sainthood, at the measure of the stature of Christ's fullness" (Eph 4:13).[139]

These common threads evident in patristic and medieval English and Bishop Hall are signposts of shared ideas. Hall was not a Protestant interloper of Tridentine spirituality but a scholar acquainted with sources of a broad stream. His understanding of the soul and the philosophical nature of knowledge added to the strength of his program and his writings. To this argument, chapter 4 will seek to address and add support.

---

139. Climacus, *Ladder of Divine Ascent*, 291.

Chapter 4

The *Art of Divine Meditation* Compared

The beginning of prayer is the expulsion of distraction from the very start by a single thought; the middle stage is the concentration on what is being said or thought; its conclusion is rapture in the Lord.

—John Climacus, seventh century

Searching out the source materials behind Hall's work is a complex trail of combining evaluations of styles, theological trajectories, and cultural influences. Looking at the English mystics of Walter Hilton and the anonymous work The Cloud of Unknowing along with the Eastern Father John Climacus, *The Art of Meditation* draws upon a diverse source of spirituality that has commonalities. This study makes the argument in favor of Bishop Hall relying upon an English and medieval tradition, specifically, Walter Hilton's *Scale of Perfection* and the anonymous author of *The Cloud of Unknowing*, rather than merely accommodating Counter-Reformation spiritual traditions. Both works represented a classic Augustinian meditative practice rooted in medieval England and applicable to both lay and cenobite audiences. The later stylistic aspect is important in that it highlights the same vein of Hall's *Art of Meditation* to be a guide for all Christian believers. The former point of having an English cultural origin, one with geographic proximity to Hall, would underscore a layer of influence for Hall and his contemporaries. It is noted that Hilton's *Scale* was republished by

John Wynkyn de Worde in 1498, a famous and prolific printer in London. Frank Huntley's source theory of Thomas a Kempis being the unknown monk that Hall made reference to in his *Art of Meditation* is an important alternative to the views that Hall was merely appropriating the source material used by Ignatius of Loyola. With these dates and the works' popularity in mind and given Hall's theology, it is not unlikely that these English mystics were sources that easily translated into spiritual guides for an English Protestant audience. This chapter argues the case that Hall was careful and deliberate in retrieving an Augustinian contemplative practice that was organically English and theologically orthodox for the broad application of Puritan piety in the seventeenth century.

LADDER OF ASCENT: TYPOLOGY OF CONTEMPLATIVE MEDITATION

Describing the spiritual journey towards a deeper love with Christ as a "ladder of ascent" was used by John Chrysostom, Gregory of Nazianzus, and Dionysius the Pseudo-Areopogate. Following these divines, John Climacus (579–649) used it and extended it as a central theme in his *Ladder of Divine Ascent*. Climacus wrote for Christians unable to travel to Mount Sinai. These sequential steps followed the upward climb in his principle masterpiece still in use by Eastern Orthodox believers.[1] It was developed on the image of thirty steps in the rungs of a ladder, each corresponding to the earthly life of Jesus up to his baptism and prior to his public ministry: in this it was Christocentric in substance and written at the request of Gregory the Great (590–604) for the help of all Christians. There is no conclusive proof that Joseph Hall appropriated Climacus's classic. However, the fact of the work's significance, its relevance for Hall's own thinking, and the fact that copies were available in the seventeenth-century to British scholars leads to the reasonable conclusion that the work influenced Hall's own. Post-Reformation English divines, especially Calvinist Conformist divines, were more willing to appropriate works from the Eastern Church than the early Protestant Reformers.[2] Moreover, John Climacus's mystical theology is consistent with

---

1. Schwanda, *Soul Recreation*, 92. Schwanda notes that the Puritan Ambrose makes reference to John Climacus in his work *Looking unto Jesus*. The use of patristic source material was undergoing a renewal in the seventeenth century. That this well-known Eastern spiritual classic was becoming accessible to English readers is not too difficult to explain since King James I made Greek Orthodox scholars welcome to London in an attempt to bring the English Church in the center of Christian thinking for the world.

2. Ford, *James Ussher*, 237–38. Bishop James Ussher was a translator of the Greek manuscripts of the *Letters of Ignatius* (35–107) and used a critical study of the Greek

The Art of Meditation.[3] Like Hall, Climacus wrote in a dialectic form, with brief sentences and clever everyday analogies. Bishop Kallistos Ware reflects on Climacus's style: "The author lives short, sharp sentences, pithy definitions, paradoxical aphorisms, for his purpose is to wake the reader up."[4] The same can be said of Joseph Hall in his style of writing. Patterns of the ascent towards beatification, while simplified in Hall, bear too much resemblance to the *Ladder of Divine Ascent*. Along with trying to find the various sources behind Hall, it is equally important to view how Hall influenced this piety of ascent.

In addition to establishing a theory of Hall's sources, this chapter looks briefly at Thomas Watson, Richard Baxter, and Jonathan Edwards as following a stream of influence that carried this tradition on in England and New England. Their work on meditative spirituality is sometimes identified as a departure from Hall by literary critics. Both Watson and Baxter directly appealed to Hall as a primary influence. Louis Bouyer speaks of Baxter's indebtedness to Hall as he wrote *The Saint's Everlasting Rest*: "Thereafter he embarks on a detailed description and warm recommendation of the best method of meditation as he sees it; and, with endearing honesty, he makes no attempt to hide from us that he has taken this method from a Puritan of the preceding generation, Joseph Hall."[5] Secondly, the role that English medieval texts had on the Protestant imagination can argue the value of exploring how Hilton's *Scale of Perfection* and the Augustinian *Cloud of Unknowing* provided key backdrops to Hall's contribution in this type of writing. Given his criticism of Jesuits and his desire to sustain a practice that would be readily welcomed and received by English Protestants, he did not need to borrow from the Counter-Reformation to achieve his stated goal: "If, then, we can by any other method work in our hearts so deep an apprehension of the matter meditated as it may duly stir the affections, it is that only we require."[6] Hall's pragmatic rule, however, did not mean he would be open to anything that denied the boundaries of Scripture or the need for a grace-dependent epistemology. It is one reason that Hall would be naturally drawn to the kind of system found in English medieval texts of Hilton and the unknown author

---

text (1644) to prove the legitimacy of the episcopacy form of government.

3. Climacus, *Ladder of Divine Ascent*, 8. "Convinced as he is of the need for encounter and participation, for direct tasting and touching, John's aim in *The Ladder* is not to inculcate abstract teaching or to impose a formal code of ascetic rules, but to evoke in his readers an experience similar to his own. As the late Fr. George Florovsky put it, '*The Ladder* is an invitation to pilgrimage.'"

4. Climacus, *Ladder of Divine Ascent*, 10.

5. Bouyer, *History of Christian Spirituality*, 158.

6. Hall, *Art*, 88–89.

of *The Cloud of Unknowing*. These two Augustinian monks were keen to put a primary emphasis upon divine grace.[7] It is another example of how Hall would not be merely dependent or confined to the spiritual tradition of the Counter-Reformation. Contemplative or ascetical theology already had a long and rich tradition in England with a wide range of influence.

TWO ENGLISH MEDIEVAL SOURCES

The concept of moving towards an experience beyond the cognitive to a "darkness of unknowing" comes as early as Dionysius the Areopogate.[8] When an Augustinian monk in the fourteenth century in Northern England wrote *The Cloud of Unknowing*, he was using the idea, with certain safeguards, that the spiritual ascent of the soul reached into an experience that moved beyond rational and speculative truth. In a sense, it steered clear of the twin dangers of mysticism of total submersion of the conscious soul, on one hand, and on the other, a model of rules with a hierarchy of Conformity. The anonymous author bears affinity with Hilton and the Eastern tradition of apophatic theology seen in the spiritual tradition of John Climacus.[9]

Walter Hilton (d. 1396) was an English mystic of an Augustinian order whose writings had an indelible influence on the piety of British people both Catholic and Protestant. Along with Richard Rolle and Julian of Norwich, Hilton was a part of a thirteenth-century spiritual tradition of pre-Reformation spirituality that favorably compares with the work of the Continental tradition of Bernard of Clairvaux and Thomas a Kempis. Secondly, with the prolific publishing effort of London book companies around the latter part of the sixteenth century, these works were more abundant and retained by British libraries.

To make a case that Walter Hilton's *The Scale of Perfection* and the unknown source of *The Cloud of Unknowing* were two leading contenders for substance, ideas, and thoughts behind Hall's work is built on two assumptions. One is the historical and cultural contexts of Hall. Both are English, Augustinian mystical authors, which, in the view of this study, would be good sources for Hall's effort in establishing the English Church as a contributing stream of medieval spirituality. In addition to the publication dates

---

7. Milosh, *Scale of Perfection*, 80. Hilton's teachings on grace are more emphatic than that of his contemporaries.

8. Pseudo-Dionysius, *Complete Works*, 1.3.

9. Thiselton, *Thiselton Companion to Christian Theology*, 247. Efforts to identify this work as being authored by Walter Hilton have not been conclusive. See also Owen, "Christian Mysticism," 31–42.

(both republished in 1494) of these two works fits the time frame that Hall cites. These would be sources well known by Hall and his contemporaries.[10]

Secondly, the words, style, and content of these early Middle English spiritual writers were clearly echoed by Hall, never by direct quotes, but rather ideological parallels. Hall did name *Rosetum* as a key influence in style, but this cannot mean a single source of influence. Hall drew upon the meditative tradition of Mauburnus and his *Rosetum*, a collection of spiritual writing including a method of contemplation that, in keeping with the Benedictine tradition of balancing prayer and work, sought to influence an active spirituality. It might be the source he drew from when he referred to an unnamed monk in his introduction to *The Art of Meditation*, the date he used would back up this claim:

> At the end of his life, Mauburnus became an abbot at the monastery of Livry near Paris, one of the monasteries he had reformed according to the precepts of the *devotio moderna*. The *Rosetum*, his most important work, is an extensive introduction to the practice of meditation... In essence, the work amounts to a full overview of the medieval tradition of spiritual exercises. At the request of his fellow brothers, Mauburnus devised a collection of systematically arranged meditation schemes on the basis of his personal *rapiarium*, preceded by a first abbreviated version published in 1491, this extensive work was printed five times between 1494 and 1620; the best-known edition was published in Paris in 1510.[11]

Mombaer was one who was building on a multiple influence of earlier sources. His *Rosetum* was a manual on prayer and contemplation and drew upon multiple sources. It exhibited "teachings not only of the exponents of the so-called *devotio moderna* but also of less recent authors such as Augustine, Bernard, Aquinas, and the Victorines, while at the same time it provided a detailed method of mystical meditation."[12] Theories of Hall's sources for his work will be further defined in chapter 5. Beyond Hall's work to his later influence upon the Protestant tradition we have plenty of

---

10. Underhill, *Cloud of Unknowing*, iv. "Then, about the middle of the fourteenth century, England—at that time in the height of her great mystical period—led the way with the first translation into vernacular of the Areopogate's work. In *Dionise Hid Divinite*, a version of the *Mystica Theologia*, this spiritual treasure-house was first made accessible to those outside the professional religious class" (Underhill, *Cloud of Unknowing*, iii). Underhill also asserts that attempts to show that Walter Hilton was the author of *The Cloud* has failed, but Hilton does, at the least, reveal a strong affinity.

11. Hasche-Burger, "Music and Meditation," 348.

12. Hughes, *Lefèvre: Pioneer of Ecclesiastical Renewal in France*, 37.

written acknowledgments. Hall was not merely translating a singular model of meditation for his contemporaries but distilling a multitude of voices from ancient sources that characterized the accessibility to and interest the seventeenth-century scholars had in Latin, Greek, and Middle-English texts in the theological libraries of the *stupor mundi* present in England. Hall also mentioned the work of Dionysius the Pseudo-Areopogate (fifth century), who predates many other sources into the patristic period, and thereby reflected a very broad casting of source material to justify Hall being called a "Calvinist Conformist."[13] It may be legitimately argued that in light of the breadth of his knowledge, for Bishop Hall, a Reformed church was the same as "one, holy, catholic, and apostolic."

This concern over the apostolic foundation was seen in the invitation of the British crown of papal delegates to see that apostolic succession of the English bishops was unbroken, and in Bishop Ussher's groundbreaking research in patristic texts to prove episcopacy in the writings of Ignatius of Antioch, which were just being discovered in the West.[14] These efforts made a case for the prelacy both on the grounds of biblical interpretation and historical extrabiblical evidence going back to the second century. This was the intellectual climate and is evidence of the sense of accessibility to sources that were not as available to early Protestant scholarship. Ussher and Hall are prime examples of English Protestants that would mine gold wherever they found true gold from patristic and medieval sources and translated these sources for contemporary consumption. The unknown writer of the famous *Cloud of Unknowing* and Hilton's *Scale of Perfection* would be not as ancient as Orthodox spiritual masters from the East, but were fine examples of Augustinian mysticism readily known and likely appreciated by Hall. Frank Huntley makes a strong case that Hall followed the spirit and affective approach of a Kempis as well as Bonaventure.[15]

---

13. Steere, "Quo Vadis?," 15.

14. Corwin, *St. Ignatius and Christianity in Antioch*, 5. The rise of textual criticism was used in positive ways to show authentic texts against interpolators from the Middle Ages. Beginning in 1623, Vedelius of Geneva would establish a reliable text based on quotations from Eusebius. A final Greek version of authentic writings was eventually published by Ruinart in 1689. This reveals the strong interest and research in the patristic period in the seventeenth century. In addition to the textual criticism, this linkage would add additional credibility to English claims of apostolic succession, more in its attesting to the role of the Church of England in continuing its catholic and doctrinal legitimacy. Both Ussher and Hall as English bishops with Reformed convictions were equally concerned about this English Catholic heritage.

15. Huntley, *Bishop Joseph Hall*, 78.

COMPARISON WITH COUNTER-REFORMATION MEDITATIVE PRACTICE[16]

Bishop Hall wrote his *Art of Meditation* in response to the growing popularity of Catholic meditative practice (found in Ignatian and Salesian methods), so the historical context of this writing is important to establish, but it does not mean to deny Hall's complex source material that offered alternatives and complemented this piety. In his historical survey of Christian spirituality, Louis Bouyer makes this assessment: "The method of the *Exercises* had ended by reducing mysticism to an ascetic system with semi-Pelagian tendencies. Whatever our views, there seems no doubt about this: that in the use to which Hall, and above all Baxter, put Ignatius's sources we find pure practical Pelagianism superimposed on a mysticism of *sola gratia*."[17] While Protestants historically have highlighted this distinction within the doctrine of justification by faith alone, it is also needed to note this difference within the sphere of the doctrine of sanctification. The tendency to fall into moralism within a pretext of a grace-initiated redemption is ever present in the spectrum of the two streams of spirituality. These two typologies of spiritual practices have been expressed historically along a spectrum of a grace and human response that presents variations between two poles, rather than clear and distinct categories. This is not to deny the importance of theological differences and doctrinal boundaries but to highlight within the practice of the discipline of meditation that these typologies are not always predictably categorized in ecclesiastical terminology. While this is demonstratively true prior to the sixteenth century, and before the intractable division resulting from the Council of Trent, it is also evident in years following in the post-Reformation traditions among Protestants and Roman Catholics. As Ozment observes, "What the Council of Trent was to the renewal and discipline of the church doctrine and institutions, the Society of Jesus became to the revival and discipline of its spirituality."[18] That other Catholic and Augustinian spiritualities continued within the post-Tridentinian church is not in question.

---

16. Baucum, "Bishop Hall and Ignatius of Loyola." This section is a reworking of the material dealing with how Hall's meditation is different in form and theology from Ignatian spirituality, even with the similar sources and continuity that existed between them.

17. Bouyer, *History of Christian Spirituality*, 159. One does not need to agree with Bouyer's conclusion on this matter, but his perception about a tendency towards Pelagianism on the part of Ignatius is accurate. His rather negative view of Baxter is stated in a similar vein: "For here 'grace' is no more than a psychological determinism set up by the Creator for the benefit of the elect, and all they need to do is discover it and set it in motion so as to obtain assurance and 'the saints' everlasting rest" (Bouyer, *History of Christian Spirituality*, 159).

18. Ozment, *Age of Reform*, 409.

The point here to see how the Ignatian method drew upon an epistemology that was different than the approach that Hall developed.

In comparing the two methods of meditation of Bishop Joseph Hall (1574–1656) and Ignatius of Loyola (1491–1556), this descriptive model will provide a heuristic way to analyze commonalities and convergences as well as distinguish the stylistic, psychological, and theological differences and departures of philosophy. Both Hall and Ignatius, both of whose works provided manuals for instructing a Christian understanding to meditation, represented two very different approaches to this ancient practice even though they shared common sources (fourteenth- and fifteen-century thinkers) and in many points shared similar language and ordering of steps. As Louis Martz argues for Hall's contribution, "Here the hint of the presence of something like innate ideas in the deep caves of the soul leads directly to a long account of what might be called the dramatic action of Augustinian meditation. It is an action significantly different from the method of meditation later set forth by Ignatius Loyola."[19] These differences are more than stylistic and cultural in nature, nor can one simply qualify them in neat ecclesiastical categories as either Protestant and Augustinian, respectively, or Roman Catholic and semi-Pelagian. Furthermore, a comparison is found in different eyes looking from opposing angles at the same mountain. Hence, while there are cultural and chronological distance between these two models of meditation, the subtle differences are substantial in a philosophical way.[20]

The next chapter will explore the underlying assumptions about the soul and its faculties that were rooted in Augustinian and Thomistic traditions that stood in contrast to a growing modern view emerging in the seventeenth century. The historical trajectory of the soul and the relationship of the imagination to the reasoning faculty is especially important in the divergence of Hall's method from the Jesuit use of sensory epistemology. In the final chapter, an argument is made that Hall provided a rich and complex view of the imagination that would have far-ranging implications for spirituality and the moral imagination of later Protestants. It is a view that questions the common perception that imaginative theology belongs to Roman Catholics and not to Protestants.

IGNATIUS OF LOYOLA: THE SPIRITUAL EXERCISES

Ignatius was a contemporary of John Calvin who entered *The College of Montaigu* in Paris the same year that Calvin, the Reformer, would graduate.

19. Martz, *Poetry of Meditation*, 22–23.
20. Baucum, "Bishop Hall and Ignatius of Loyola," 2–4.

There is no evidence that the two ever met.[21] Their respective paths would take them in very different directions, but both would be influential reforming lights for their causes. In one way, Ignatius represented the embodiment of the goals of the Counter-Reformation, not as a theologian of the church but as a leader of personal piety and the spiritual renewal of a church corrupted by centuries of worldly clergy and rampant immorality among the baptized. Historian Steven Ozment raises the important question, "Why did an effective Catholic lay spirituality have to await the formation of the Society of Jesus and the work of the Council of Trent in the mid-sixteenth century?"[22] It is a question worth pondering.

Born in northern Spain in 1491 to the noble family of Loyola, Ignatius grew up in the Basque world of romance, music, and the canons of chivalry. Like Cervantes's old knight Don Quixote, Ignatius was witnessing the passing of an old-world order of feudal Spain, full of noble virtues and respect for rules of order and class. He was trained more for the court and knighthood than for the role of a cleric or a spiritual leader. However, his worldly endeavors would be cut short by the blast of a cannon ball in a battle against French forces in Pamplona in 1521. The months the Spaniard spent in recovery at a hospital in painful traction would provide time for spiritual reflection and mark a point of religious conversion when he was twenty-six years old. While convalescing from his battle wounds and longing to read books of romance, he discovered two medieval books that laid a foundation for a spiritual appetite. The first was a collection of the lives of saints known as *The Golden Legend* as well as the *Vita Christi* by Carthusian monk Ludolph of Saxony.[23] The latter work received wide readership in the Augustinian monastery in Erfurt, where Luther was a monk.[24] In 1522 he was given a copy of *Exercises for the Spiritual Life* by Garcia de Cisneros, abbot of Montserrat. The first outline of his own *Spiritual Exercises* was written in rough form in this year of spiritual awakening. Another key pivotal experience was a vision he had of the Holy Trinity which was seen like three musical notes and gave him a "new understanding" of Christ.[25] This practice of contemplation would have

---

21. Greef, *Writings of John Calvin*, 4.

22. Ozment, *Age of Reform*, 397.

23. Ozment, *Age of Reform*, 410. "During his lengthy convalescence in Loyola, he became absorbed in two religious classics: Ludolphus of Saxony's *Life of Christ* and a collection of saint's lives known as *The Golden Legend* (*flos sanctorum*). Later, Thomas a Kempis's *Imitation of Christ* became his favorite book."

24. Oberman, *Dawn of the Reformation*, 70–71.

25. Ignatius of Loyola, *Ignatius of Loyola*, 27. Using his autobiography, the editors show how Ignatius recounts his own words of this experience: "The eyes of his understanding began to be opened; not that he saw any vision, but he understood and learned

a formative influence in his *Exercises*. Seeking to follow in the steps of Christ, Ignatius went on a pilgrimage to Jerusalem in 1523, but returned to Barcelona to begin his training in Latin at the age of thirty-three. Eventually, Ignatius would enroll in the College of Montaigu in 1528, joining students less than half his age. In Paris, the former soldier and Spanish pilgrim attended the school where Jean Gerson once taught and where the *devotio moderna* flourished. It was the same school where Erasmus and Rabelais had studied a decade earlier, and he acquired a humanist and classical orientation to their thought. After completing his studies at the college, Ignatius attended lectures at a Dominican convent in Paris where he brought his Bible and Peter Lombard's *Sentences*. It was a significant feature of his training in Paris. "Ignatius's formation was basically Thomistic, and he conceived his preferential affection for St. Thomas, which later led him to prescribe 'the scholastic doctrine of St. Thomas's for the scholastics of his Society . . . He also indicated his esteem for Peter Lombard."[26] The strictness of his style would be one evidence for this dominant theme inherited from Aquinas and Lombard. Here one can see ideas more semi-Pelagian than of an Augustinian view of grace and the condition of the soul. Ignatius not only prescribed a detailed method that was to be used by members of his Society during a month of devotion, but he also showed this approach in his *Spiritual Diaries* by giving examples of his own personal experience in using his *Exercises*. This provides helpful insights in the kind of experience he had in his practice of the *Exercises* and what he might expect from others. There seemed to be little room for much variance in either application of the steps or the desired outcome.[27] Without a doubt conformity has its value for a systematic development. However, one

---

many things, both spiritual matters and matters of faith and of scholarship, and this with so great an enlightenment that everything seemed new to him." So Ignatius, in reflecting on his experience years later, is not preoccupied with the particular "vision" but with its effects. "Ignatius's experiences were not merely corporeal visions, by which a mystic gaze on an object whether real or apparent, outside of himself or herself; nor were they merely imaginative visions in which God so affects a mystic's imagination or 'picturing faculty' that he or she sees an object not really present . . . [the visions] were predominantly intellectual visions, insights, in which God communicates himself in a way that leads a mystic to a better understanding of truths" (Ignatius of Loyola, *Ignatius of Loyola*, 30).

26. Ignatius of Loyola, *Spiritual Exercises*, 37.

27. Ignatius of Loyola, *Spiritual Exercises*, §19. It is advised in the introductory section called "Notations" that instructions be given to allow some variance and application for those who work secular jobs: "One who is educated or talented, but engaged in public affairs or necessary business, should take an hour and a half daily for the *Spiritual Exercises*" (Ignatius of Loyola, *Ignatius of Loyola*, 30). There are other ways one can adapt the steps, but it is stated as a caveat, that the same desired outcome will not be the same!

judges that this distinctive approach, as well as the examples he gives, reflect a consistent method that he used for contemplation and application of the affections. On one entry in his diary for Ash Wednesday he wrote,

> Upon entering the chapel, during prayer I perceived deeply in my heart, or more precisely I saw beyond my natural powers, the Most Holy Trinity and Jesus. He was representing me, or placing me, or serving as my mediator with the Most Holy Trinity in order that intellectual vision might be granted me. At this perception and sight I was covered with tears and love terminating chiefly on Jesus. Toward the Trinity too I felt a respect of affectionate awe closer to reverential love than to anything else.[28]

It is clear from this and other entries that the heart of *caritas* and a response of tears was for Ignatius a primary goal of meditation. His *Exercises* were a complex mixture of Scripture, prayer, contemplation, and variations of steps and repetition aimed at moving the affections in a purer love for God. As Steven Ozment notes,

> The *Spiritual Exercises* built most perceptively on the interconnection of emotion, belief, and behavior. What justification by faith had attempted to accomplish for the anguished Protestant saint, Ignatius's disciplined exercises tried to do for the troubled Catholic saint. The routines it prescribed overcame old habits and prepared individuals for new states of mind and morality by playing directly on their basic emotions of fear and love. Particular sins, for example, were eliminated by attacking each with all five senses and the mind's power of imagination at regular daily intervals.[29]

The idea of sensory-based knowledge has a long history in philosophical discussion through the medieval period. Long before John Locke's empirically-based epistemology took the philosophical world by storm, the role of the senses and the faculties of the soul had been a key question moving from Augustine to the refinement of the discussions in those who followed Aquinas. The important theological idea to keep in mind is the inability of natural senses to give adequate knowledge to experience God apart from grace. Sensory-based knowledge is tainted and can be distorted, as will be further elucidated later in chapter 5. Another example of this sensory-based imagination is seen in St. Teresa's *Inward Castle*, a work that would be influential in England.

---

28. Ignatius, *Ignatius of Loyola*, 251.
29. Ozment, *Age of Reform*, 412.

ST. TERESA OF AVILA (1515–82): INWARD DESCENT

The English edition of Teresa's *Vida* was published in London in 1623, and a Dutch translation came out in 1642, translated by Sir Tobie Matthew. The later edition made a sensation in England and was the inspiration behind Richard Crenshaw's serial poem on Teresa coming out in 1646 and 1648. This may reveal, among many connections, broad readership and vast appeal the Spanish tradition had for the English public even if popular sentiments against the Jesuits was also present. This patchwork of theological and spiritual traditions was part and parcel of the cosmopolitan landscape of London. It may reflect the long Augustinian spirituality that England already possessed within her shores. Teresa was a Carmelite nun who saw her vocation as reforming an order that had a tradition coming from the thirteenth century at Mount Carmel as a result of the Second Crusade. Its rule was austere and hermit-like in simplicity.[30] As a reforming movement, the new order was not well received, and the leading hermit, John of the Cross, was imprisoned and Teresa was confined in her room by the Inquisition. At times many of her writings were controversial among the Counter-Reformation, and the *Inquisition* was suspicious of her ecstatic visions as the rest of those who stressed private piety. They were known as *alumbrados*—the spirituals.[31] She is well known for her many works, including *The Way of Perfection* (1562) and her famous *Interior Castle*. While at times under suspicion of heresy by Rome, she was eventually canonized and designated as a Doctor of the Church.[32]

A manual on the Christian life written by the Dutch humanist, Desiderius Erasmus entitled the *Enchiridion* was immensely popular in Spain and aided the efforts towards a moral reformation that was embraced by Charles I of Spain. Teresa had read Bernardino de Laredo's *The Ascent of Mount Zion* and Alonso de Madrid's *The Art of Serving God*; hence the emphasis on private prayer and devotion was well established in Spain and receptive to an English piety. The appreciation for the work of Teresa lingered on even into the nineteenth century as attested by the Scottish pastor Alexander Whyte, who wrote *Santa Teresa: An Appreciation* (1898).[33] The cross-currents of this contemplative piety is, as such, a mosaic of different sources crossing the English Channel. This kind of back-and forth influence did not end in the later years of the seventeenth century; as books became more dominant

---

30. Rapley, *Lord Is Their Portion*, 138.

31. Rapley, *Lord Is Their Portion*, 141. Teresa's spiritual biography, *Vida*, was not published until after her death.

32. Thiselton, *Thiselton Companion to Christian Theology*, 806.

33. Whyte, *Santa Teresa*. It is noteworthy that an evangelical Calvinist would have the appreciation of such a wide and diverse spectrum of spirituality.

and accessible, it would become even more complex. Later English Puritans were not isolationists in their use of materials, even given their commitment to Reformed orthodoxy. In accessing the legacy of Hall, it is this thesis that later Puritans found in Hall not only a champion of ascetical piety, but a faithful exponent of a praxis rooted in grace and guided by Reformed assumptions of revelation.

BISHOP HALL'S INFLUENCE AMONG THE PURITANS

Hall began writing his devotional works after William Perkins and William Ames[34] had seen their publications form a growing movement of Reformed orthodox piety. Joseph Hall, writing his *Art of Meditation* and publishing in 1603, represented the beginning of a second wave of Puritan writers of the Caroline period. Richard Hooker in his magisterial and defining work for the Church of England, *Ecclesiastical Laws*, frequently took aim at Puritans and was never complimentary of their influence, but this is against the backdrop of Hooker's ongoing defense of Cranmer's theological vision to bring the Church of England to a unity of classical Reformed faith.[35] That Perkins and Ames were critical of Elizabethan compromises on some issues and heavy-handed on Conformity made the term "Puritan" arguably more of a term of negative connotation in reference to the established church and not on core orthodox doctrine. It is an ongoing and complex question, but for this study in assessing Hall's historical context, it is seen, as previously stated, that Bishop Hall held on to both polar elements; of being a Calvinist in doctrine and piety and the other pole as a loyal churchman. It proved to be an increasingly untenable position to take with a religious war on the horizon. His personal commitment and professional integrity was widely known and respected by most, except for the extreme elements of both parties. Thomas Watson was one who respected Hall and emulated his work. While not alone, he stood as one representative whose work on meditation was read and appreciated.[36]

---

34. Ambrose would spend thirty days every year on a wilderness retreat in meditation; see Schwanda, *Soul Recreation*, Appendix. This practice underscores the role of both types of meditation, intentional or deliberate and occasional meditation, especially as the latter is engaged in the interaction of the natural world. This would also be true for Jonathan Edwards's spiritual contemplations in the outdoors. This was a theme deeply etched in the Puritan imagination of New England, which in an extreme form is found in Emerson's Transcendentalism.

35. Hooker, in *Of the Laws of Ecclesiastical Polity*, gives an extended and detailed defense of the doctrine of justification by faith alone, and also asserts the authority of Scripture as final in matters of doctrine, both key hinge doctrines for Reformed theology.

36. Schwanda, "Sweetness in Communion with God," 35. Schwanda prefers to call

Thomas Watson

The wider lines of influence are seen in the work of Thomas Watson, where his own book *A Treatise on Meditation* includes a foreword by Edward Reynolds with a laudatory mention of Hall: "Though some learned men of former times have written some things upon this subject, yet, of our age and in our language, I do not remember any who have purposely handled it but Seneca and the learned and reverend Bishop Hall."[37] Again Hall was singled out as "English Seneca" who set new standards for devotional writing.[38] The idea of influence for contemporary readers will be addressed near the conclusion, but for now it is important for a proper understanding of Hall's forming methodology to look at some of the historical conditions in which he wrote and how he would be received in Stuart England in the dawn of the seventeenth century. When Thomas Watson studied at Christ's College, the principle master was Richard Holdsworth, who provided these Cambridge students guides for reading so "that you may increase in Piety and saving knowledge as well as in humane learning," which included the works of Bishop Joseph Hall, Richard Sibbes, John Davenant and William Perkins.[39]

Watson's work on meditation, entitled *The Christian on the Mount* (1657), bears many similar themes and concepts to Hall's treatise. It was shorter in length with eighteen small chapters, the steps of meditation contained only six rules (compared to Hall's seventeen), and the work was arranged slightly differently, with many of the contexts and explanations of meditation taken up after the rules were given. Substantially in themes and inclusion of occasional meditations, the two works belong to the same tradition. Watson is, as Edwards Reynolds suggested, standing on the shoulders of Hall, whose work was singular in its reception in the English world but not readily assessible for reasons not fully identified. Reynolds, for example, made a veiled reference only to Hall's voluminous work.[40] Compared to early medieval texts, Hall's book was a simplification, but Watson was even more

---

the Puritan stream of mysticism "contemplative-mystical piety," a term that his helpful and clarifies a specific stream of spirituality rooted in the medieval Christian world that also avoids the more Neoplatonic connotations of other streams found in German and non-Christian spiritual practice.

37. Watson, *Christian on the Mount*, xii.
38. Smith, "Bishop Hall: 'Our English Seneca,'" 1191–1204.
39. Schwanda, "Sweetness in Communion with God," 57.
40. Watson, *Christian on the Mount*, xii. If in Reynold's day the copy of Hall's *Art of Meditation* was to be found in his multivolume work, then the mere fact that this was a simple guide for the average Christian would make it less available and user-friendly. This might be one factor. The historical context of Hall's writings would also make him more of an influencer than a wider and more popular author.

adaptable for the average reader. Watson quoted from Gregory Nazianzen, Augustine, Bernard, Bonaventure, and even Ignatius of Loyola.[41] These sources were known and incorporated by Hall, thereby reflecting the ongoing tradition that Hall used and not departing from it. In Watson's chapter "The Excellence of Meditation," he made several references and allusions to other sources. In some of these references, we see a broad spectrum of authors.

> Aristotle places felicity in the contemplation of the mind. Meditation is highly commended by Augustine, Chrysostom, and Cyprian as the nursery of piety. Jerome calls it his paradise. With what words shall I set it forth? Other duties have done excellently, but you excel them all. Meditation is a friend to all the graces; it helps water the plantation.[42] I may call it, in Basil's expression, the treasury where all the graces are locked up, and, with Theophylact, the gate and portal by which we enter into glory. By meditation the spirits are raised and heightened to a kind of angelic frame.[43] Meditation sweetly puts us in heaven before we arrive there. Meditation brings God and the Soul together. Meditation is the saints' looking glass, by which they see things invisible.[44] Meditation is the golden ladder by which they ascend to paradise.[45] Meditation is the spy they send abroad to search the land of promise, and it brings a cluster of the grapes of Eschol with it. In each of these are biblical allusions. Meditation is the dove they send out, and it brings an olive branch of peace in its mouth.[46]

Like Hall, Watson borrowed from ancient wisdom to reinforce the biblical view of meditation. Watson admitted and affirmed how he was indebted to Hall in offering others a manual that was both easy and flexible for the average layman.

---

41. Watson, *Christian on the Mount*, 108. He quotes Ignatius: "Christ, my love, is crucified."

42. St. Teresa, the Spanish mystic and nun, used the imagery of watering a garden in her treatise on prayer. See Medwick, *Teresa of Avila*, 99. Written in 1563, Watson's *Christian on the Mount* would be known in England. "With God's help, we have to make these plants grow, as good gardeners do, watering them carefully so that they don't die but begin producing flowers, which give off an appealing scent, to delight this Lord of ours."

43. Hilton, *Scale of Perfection*, 301.

44. Underhill, *Cloud of Unknowing*, 62.

45. Climacus, *Ladder of Divine Ascent*, was translated into Latin in the eleventh century, and another version was translated in the fourteenth century by the Francisian Angelus Clarenus. See Climacus, *Ladder of Divine Ascent*, 68.

46. Watson, *Christian on the Mount*, 92.

Richard Baxter as a Calvinist Ascetic

It was the English and Puritan-minded minister of Kiddminster, Richard Baxter, that revealed in his writings substantial credit to Hall. Principally, Baxter was influenced by *The Art of Meditation* in many of his works, but explicitly in the fourth part of *The Saint's Everlasting Rest* (1650).[47] It was this work where there is an unmistakable approach to meditation drawn from Hall—which the interior work of the soul towards the love of God was more important than an external display of pious works.[48] Baxter was also aware of the ongoing influence of the piety of the Counter-Reformation in England. He critiqued the Jesuit's approach as "nothing but a pleading of the case with our own souls."[49] As Huntley observes in the works of Baxter, he shows "an unveiled thrust at *The Spiritual Exercises*," writing: "They have thought that Meditation is nothing but the bare thinking of Truths, and the rolling of them in the Understanding and Memory."[50] The irenic spirit of Bishop Hall was also seen in Baxter in times when a moderate approach was easily dismissed: perhaps a reason why an advocate of "a mere Christianity" followed in the trail of Hall's advocacy as an "Ecumenical Calvinist Churchman."[51] So it is evident that both Hall and Baxter took a middle position regarding Conformity that was increasingly at odds with the *Sitz im Leben* of the civil war. However, the unity they sought was more spiritual in its essence. "The Augustinian devotional tradition, so firmly rooted in Scripture, bound Puritan spirituality to the practices of other parties in seventeenth-century England. While raging theological and ecclesiological conflicts divided Christians, religious experiences in the practice of the devotional life were remarkably similar."[52] True, there were many similarities and source-borrowing, but there were also differences, and these distinctions need to be studied considering the historical development and philosophical background to better grasp the contours of a trajectory of influence.

Leading scholar on spiritual writers Louis Bouyer makes clear that Baxter was directly influenced by Hall's *Art of Meditation*. "Thereafter he embarks on a detailed description and warm recommendation of the best method of meditation as he sees it; and, with endearing honesty, he makes

---

47. In Baxter's *Saint's Everlasting Rest*, Part 4, he deals with the Christian duty in meditation and quotes Hall's work, often referring to his *Soliloquy*, and uses his Latin translation.

48. Baxter, *Saint's Everlasting Rest*, 475. He cites a lengthy quote from Hall.

49. Huntley, *Bishop Joseph Hall*, 100.

50. Huntley, *Bishop Joseph Hall*, 100.

51. Dewar, "Bishop Joseph Hall," 5.

52. Hambrick-Stowe, *Practice of Piety*, 36.

no attempt to hide from us that he has taken this method from a Puritan of the preceding generation, Joseph Hall, who had been Bishop successively of Exeter and Norwich before his suspension by Laud in 1641."[53] If Baxter has such a positive view of Hall's method and praises its worth, why would he not state his philosophical departure? That he did not state directly or indirectly any shift from him should reflect that Baxter stood in Hall's line of influence, even though the latter became more widely known and loved in England and in the American colonies.

Besides influencing Richard Baxter, *The Art of Meditation* was very popular in the American colonies despite it never being published in New England (four editions were published in Britain). Books came in many shipments over the Atlantic Ocean from England to the colonies. "Baxter's works, especially *The Saint's Everlasting Rest* (London, 1652), and those of Bishop Joseph Hall on methods of meditation and prayer, were widely read in New England in the second half of the seventeenth century."[54] The writing of manuals and guides for Christian living became commonplace in New England, and it is highly probable that Hall's method contributed to this type of literature. There are also debates over two lines of thought about Hall's meditative model among twentieth-century literary scholars, which bears some mention, but not as an extensive discussion for the present study.[55]

U. Milo Kaufmann's theory of Hall's line is that the bishop had a major influence on many Puritans, but only those who diminished the role of the imagination.[56] In Kauffman's view the Puritan strain of piety was tied more to an intellectualist model of faith. He does not include Baxter in the line of Hall, nor does he affirm the way *The Art of Meditation* established a more Augustinian psychology and orthodox view the soul's faculties. It is not clear why Baxter is understood to be an exception with a distinct departure from Hall if the nature of Hall's occasional meditations is taken in full theological context. As a literary scholar, it was not Kaufmann's focus to describe the details of the theological history of this area and subset of epistemology. Nevertheless, students of Joseph Hall are deeply indebted to both Kaufmann and Martz even if they place Hall in a line of meditation that tended to be in their view a restricted and scholastic turn. Here one can, arguably, see a certain bias that doesn't reflect fully the complete significance

---

53. Bouyer, *History of Christian Spirituality*, 158.

54. Hambrick-Stowe, *Practice of Piety*, 38.

55. Martz and Kaufman believe that Baxter is a departure from Hall and employs a more imaginative prose and style than found in Hall. See Martz, *Poetry of Meditation*, 125; Kaufmann, *Pilgrim's Progress*, 163. For a view that is different see also McCabe, *Joseph Hall*, 175.

56. Kaufmann, *Pilgrim's Progress*, 163.

that Bishop Hall had on the meditative tradition: Here is an example of the view of Kaufmann's assessment:

> Hall's treatise on meditation represents a carefully reasoned implementation of the orientation toward logos in the area of private devotion. Louis Martz, in *The Poetry of Meditation*, shows that Hall deviates from the Ignatian tradition by making no provision for the use of the imagination in meditation, goes back to the pre-Ignatian Catholic writer Joannes Mauburnus (Jean Mombaer) in order to construct a program for exciting the affections toward holy ends. Mauburnus had borrowed in turn from the *Scala Meditationis* of Johan Wessel Gansfort.[57]

While it is true that Hall was influenced by the tradition of Mauburnus's ladder of contemplations and the *Scala Meditationis*, his engagement of the imagination was positively more affirming in the use of occasional meditation and less restrictive in terms of the practitioner having the freedom to choose topics of meditation and the positive role of the imagination.

Jean Mombaer was a part of the *Brethren of the Common Life* and was referred to as "one of the restorers of almost innumerable community houses to holier living" by Lefevre in 1505.[58] Hall made a reference to an unnamed monk from whom he drew much of his ideas on the art of meditation.[59] Most assume it is primarily Mauburnus, partly because of the marginalia reference to Mauburnus and also the dating of his *Scala* in 1494.[60] While both Hall and Ignatius drew in part from this same source material, it is the view of Kaufmann that Hall was modifying the Ignatian method and adapting it for a Reformed context. Hence, the argument of Kauffman and

---

57. Kaufmann, *Pilgrim's Progress*, 121. Kaufmann represents a view on Hall that carried the notion that Hall's method was less imaginative than the Ignatian model, which is refuted by both Huntley and McCabe, two more recent scholars specializing in Bishop Hall. Kaufmann was a student of Martz who first stated the view of Hall's more rationalist, even scholastic, turn. This view is now, in my opinion, discredited, even though Martz's monumental work on Hall is without question a fine work of scholarship and pioneering in the field of Joseph Hall studies. See McCabe, *Joseph Hall*, 183, where McCabe makes a very strong case that Gerson and the *devotio moderna* had a formative influence upon Hall.

58. Hughes, *Lefèvre*, 37.

59. Hughes, *Lefèvre*, 37. "In 1510 an edition of Mauburnus's *Rosetum*, which had originally appeared in 1494, was published by Josse Bade at Lefevre's instigation. Bade, who had himself been a pupil of the Brethren of the Common Life at Ghent, and whose press was used for the printing of many important works, had previously, in 1500, brought out the works of Thomas a Kempis. He would also print Lefevre's 1514 edition of Nicholas Cusa" (Hughes, *Lefèvre*, 37).

60. This was 112 years after Joseph Hall's first edition and fits with the timeline of this reference. Huntley, *Bishop Joseph Hall*, 28.

Martz is that Hall followed a restricted role of the imagination, and Baxter and Bunyan were more open to the use of the imagination. So, the two lines in Puritan meditation, according to this theory, developed along these two distinct approaches regarding the imagination. Source use and the role of tradition does determine the argument of this particular thesis. It is the view of this study that the complexity of Hall's sources, in part, show that he had a much more nuanced approach to meditation than that allowed by Kauffman.

Frank Huntley likewise argues the literary case for this added complexity, arguing that Thomas a Kempis (rather than Mombaer) was the chief influence.[61] He argues this on the basis of Hall's style and the fact that a Kempis's authorship was not a settled question. There was a republication of the *Imitation* in 1494, which would correspond to Hall's enigmatic date reference. Yet there are others, as this study contends, that could qualify as a key reference point for Hall on precisely these same grounds.

In addition to the meditative traditions that follow the imagery of "scales and ladders," the argument that those writers came from English spiritual mystics, as set forth by David Knowles, would be readily known and therefore heavily influential in the popular mind of the people that Hall was addressing.[62] Putting these elements together does not completely solve the puzzle of Hall's sources, but it provides a more complex picture of possible texts and thinking that might have been at Hall's disposal in offering not so much a *Reformed* version of an Ignatian/Catholic practice but a more deeply Augustinian, English, and practical approach that could be both personally enriching and ecclesiastically amenable to an English Calvinist spirituality and indeed to the mainstream of Puritan piety.

---

61. Huntley, *Bishop Joseph Hall*, 29.

62. Knowles, *English Mystical Tradition*, 189. Knowles sets forth the argument that the English mystical writers were of a different type than the Spanish and German traditions. England, partly by isolation, drew upon early traditions and grew into a uniquely British mystical tradition not as well known as the others. "Yet though in fact the English stream was not destined to swell to a rive the two writers of greatest influence, the author of *The Cloud* and Hilton, for a stage in the tradition which is not represented in any other country . . . the two writers just mentioned stand midway between the unmethodical and uncoordinated teaching of the German mystics and the definitive system of theory and practice elaborated by the Spaniards." This thesis is where this study builds upon the notion that Hall would readily draw upon this English stream of medieval piety as his main sources. He was aware of the broader spectrum of traditions, but he need not be considered as placed in a way just borrowing and contextualizing other traditions. He had English, Catholic, and patristic sources to set forth his program of renewing the spiritual practice of seventeenth-century English laity.

Chapter 5

Hall's Use of Tradition on the Soul and Its Faculties

Reason, even when supported by the senses, has short wings.

—Dante, *Paradiso*

As the sources of Hall's work reveal his retrieval of medieval thought and as a translator of these ideas for his context, the last chapter establishes his comprehensive and ecumenical reach. *The Art of Meditation* was reflective of Hall's use of a long historic discourse on the nature of the soul. The rationale that Hall was reflecting not only shared resources but also a point of discontinuity with Counter-Reformation spirituality is continued in this chapter, albeit more in his view of the soul. It is beyond the scope of this study to focus on the details of theological anthropology, but identifying some concepts and ideas behind Hall's language would add clarity to this discussion. Generally stated, Hall stood in an Augustinian view of the soul that was nuanced by Aquinas and framed by Reformed orthodoxy with a richness often not fully recognized. It is not easily classified as anthropology couched in the confines of nominalism. Beyond the key sources that Hall quoted, such as Gerson and Bonaventure, this chapter will review the source history of this theological tradition. Secondly, this chapter will examine Hall's background as an interpreter of English medieval piety, particularly as it pertains to the practice of meditation as an engagement in the soul. This discussion is important to lay a foundation of thinking about the role of the imagination and how the taxonomy of the terminology can be understood contextually in the seventeenth century. The debate about the positive and negative use of the imagination is vitally important to distinguish Hall within a trajectory of Reformed orthodoxy, even with the variety of views that were held among Protestants regarding inward images and the inclination towards idolization, that is, the negative use of the imagination. The side issue of the Reformed orthodox cautions about idolatry will be noted but not with the intent of answering the difficulties of the debate; both historically and the contemporary relevance of the second commandment is not a central concern of this study.

The argument set forth in this chapter is the redeemed use of the imagination as a function in the soul that is especially important in meditation; this is especially evident in how Hall understands the created world and conscience as potentially valid mediums of grace under the final and ultimate guide of biblical revelation. As previously stated, in Hall's occasional meditations, there are deeper implications of his appropriation of metaphors drawn from nature and common life as a positive use of an enlightened imagination. Hall did not embrace a natural theology that was from below, working from sensory experience and innate truth, but one that put an emphasis on divine grace and a transcendent revelatory knowledge. In this way he represented the best of Protestant orthodoxy in placing importance on both common and special revelation within their proper spheres. In addition to the epistemological issues, it is important to discuss how Hall understood the complexity of the soul's faculties in the appropriation of knowledge, for truth is more than propositional ideas and the rational part of the mind is only one singular aspect of the human soul's totality of being.

It is part of this study's argument that Hall built upon a rich tradition of medieval discussions of the soul and its attempt to identify faculties and powers related to human experience towards God. A brief overview of this discussion is valuable for placing Hall's *Art* in historical context for the language of the soul. The Puritan contribution to faculty psychology was formed from the centuries of thinking about the soul in relationship to God. Indeed, the Christological debates in the early centuries were in part the discussion of the essence of being and the analogical connection of the human soul reflecting the triad of divine essence. For the patristic period, as later Eastern Orthodoxy still exhibits, this Trinitarian doctrine was never a separate issue from liturgy and prayer.

THE ARCHITECTURE OF THE SOUL

Behold Thou has hadst addressed an earth for use, a heaven for contemplation.[1]

The view of the soul predominating in the medieval period, and the retrieval of this psychology in the seventeenth century is evident in Hall's work on both kinds of meditation, occasional and deliberate. The human soul understood by medieval scholasticism was both mysterious and complex. Yet this complexity invited the greatest thinkers of the ages to explore and map out the intricacies of this inner space, to define and describe the architecture of its design and functions. Plato, Aristotle, Augustine, and Aquinas laid down the principles of faculty psychology that are still defining discussions of theological anthropology. The point here is that Hall reflected this discussion rather richly and often without citing sources. The soul is the very identity of the human person that is both created and mysteriously unique. That is, the real person we are and the true essence of our personality and complete identity that makes us who "we are" as so infinitely different from every other person in the vast universe of billions is that we are created as *nephesh*—"living souls." The one unifying aspect of creatureliness that makes humans distinctive among all other creatures is that they were created in the image of God—*imago Dei*. The human soul constitutes the uniqueness of reflecting God's image, its dreams and past; the noncorporeal aspects also correspond to the physical bodies that live, touch, sense, and eat, love and experience pain, hurt and grow old with age. The part of who human beings are, that spend so much time grooming to look right before others, making sure it is feed and kept, is the physical body, the corporeal part. Reformed orthodox theology never diminished the importance of the physical body, as the doctrines of the incarnation and the resurrection decidedly affirm as part of God's creative and redemptive order of our reality. The final chapter will explore the issue of senses in the practice of meditation, but it is important to note the connection of the soul to sensory knowledge and avoid a hard dualism that separates the two.[2] If the soul can be compared to architecture, then the intentional design and complexity of English Gothic cathedrals is a helpful analogy. One of the great examples of English medieval expression is the construction of the great cathedral in

---

1. Hall, *Contemplations on the Historical Passages*, 4.
2. Philosopher Kevin Corcoran states that Aquinas held to a "compound dualist view" of the soul and body, which is to say, "a human person is a soul-body composite" (Corcoran, *Rethinking Human Nature*, 37). This is a discussion dealing with contemporary debates relating to theological anthropology, an issue not of great concern here other than to note this ongoing controversy.

Salisbury and the bishopric of a fellow friend and theological kinsmen of Joseph Hall.

John Davenant (1572–1641), Bishop of Salisbury, was a fellow delegate to the Synod of Dordt who, like Hall, was committed to the vision of Reformed theology and Royalist ecclesiology. The Salisbury Cathedral, where Davenant presided, is still today a wonder of architectural achievement and English craftsmanship, constructed in a relatively short time (1220–58).[3] Like a supreme example of Gothic design, the large nave is surrounded by smaller chapels and passageways. Its vastness allowed a complexity of use and diverse space for prayer, liturgy, sacraments, and religious service to the diocese in Wiltshire. Located near the heart of old Sarum, the birthplace of the English, the Salisbury cathedral is an emblem of the complexity of the human soul reflected in its very structure. Like cathedrals, there is a unique architecture to the inner design of the soul as understood by Hall. Its tall spire pointing heavenward, and with its high arches, was built to project the soul upwards to God, towards an emphasis upon the transcendence of glory. This approach to the soul in ascent to heavenly reality was the worldview undergirding English piety and, arguably, Hall. It is evident that Hall was both familiar with the medieval appreciation of the soul and the centuries of development in thinking about the complexity of the soul's faculties.[4] This appreciation of the soul's functional parts revealed a rich texture of relationship within the faculties, not tightly systematized and logical in sequence, but working harmoniously like instruments in a symphony. His meditation on "A Pair of Spectacles" illustrates this view:

> I look upon this not as objects but as helps; as not meaning that my sight should rest in them but pass through them and by their aid discern some other things which I desire to see. Many such glasses of my soul hath and useth: I look through the glass of the creatures at the power and wisdom of their maker; I look through the glass of the Scriptures at the great mystery

---

3. The cathedral's spire is the tallest in England. The cathedral at Norwich, where Hall presided, was the second highest spire. It is a secondary note that medieval architecture had deep cultural and spiritual significance upon the English mind. Yet, the larger context of English medieval spiritual traditions that go back centuries puts forth the argument of the latent and even organic nature of the sources in Hall's inspiration and use.

4. Huntley, *Bishop Joseph Hall*, 126. Huntley writes concerning his sources that Hall drew both from ancient sources and the current literature of the day, as Huntley recounts: "He alludes to and quotes Persius, Martial, Juvenal, Aristotle's *Ethics* as well as the *Politics*, Macrobuis, Pliny, Horace's *Ars Poetica*, Suetonius, Lactantius, Plautus . . . Several times he quotes Hooker, Bacon and Sandys. He had read Donne's Pseudo-Martyr, Sidney's *Defense of Posey*, Ben Jonson's *Catiline*, du Moulin, Meric Casaubon, Sir David Lindsey, Hugo Grotius . . . and a host of others."

of redemption and the glory of an heavenly inheritance; I look through God's favors at His infinite mercy, through His judgments at His incomprehensible justice. But as these spectacles of mine presuppose a faculty in the eye and cannot give me sight when I want it but only clear that sight which I have, no more can these glasses of the creatures, of Scriptures, of favors and judgments enable me to apprehend those blessed objects except I have an eye of faith whereto they may be presented. These helps to an unbelieving man are but as spectacles to the blind. As the nature eyes, so the spiritual have their degrees of dimness, but I have ill improved my age if, as my natural eyes decay, my spiritual eye be not cleared and confirmed. But at my best I shall never but need spectacles till I come to see as I am seen [1 Cor 13:12].[5]

Like spectacles, the faculties of the soul are to be "seen through" enabling the functionality of seeing, but sight is not focused on the means, but on the object of beholding. It is a similar thought as expressed by C. S. Lewis in "Meditation in the Toolshed." As in Hall's occasional meditations, he took an ordinary experience of being in a toolshed and seeing a beam of light break through and reflected upon this as a way of thinking and knowing about truth and reality from the inside.[6] This is according to Lewis the difference between medieval and modern thought.

> But it is perfectly easy to go on all your life-giving explanations of religion, love, morality, honour, and the like, without having been inside any of them. And if you do that, you are simply playing with counters. You go on explaining a thing without knowing what it is. That is why a great deal of contemporary thought is, strictly speaking, thought about nothing—all the apparatus of thought busily working in a vacuum.[7]

Hall's ideas about the practice of meditation and the role of understanding as experiential in nature highlight that he may be considered more of a medievalist. Hall's use of the imagination was enriched by a long tradition of Augustinian spirituality that is informed by both Calvinism and against the backdrop of the restrictive regimen of Ignatian spiritual meditation. This can

---

5. Huntley, *Bishop Joseph Hall*, 181.
6. Lewis, *God in the Dock*, 212. "I was standing today in the dark toolshed. The sun was shining outside and through the crack at the top of the door there came a sunbeam. From where I stood that beam of light, with the specks of dust floating in it, was the most striking thing in the place. Everything else was almost pitch-black. I was seeing the beam, not seeing things by it."
7. Lewis, *God in the Dock*, 214.

also be seen in those who are influenced by Hall. Isaac Ambrose, Richard Baxter, and Thomas Watson reflect in their work and style Hall's influence, as has been widely understood. These authors wrote their own work of meditation and guides, but assessing Hall moves beyond just the type of literature presented by those writers. It will be argued in the next sections that Hall's literary influence had a way of shaping a whole approach towards the imagination that moved in different areas of styles and disciplines. Hence, Hall's contribution as a leading aesthetical thinker that placed Protestant and Puritan authors in making positive use of the natural world will be established. A broader appeal to the role of affective theology and Hall's methodology was seen in Sir Thomas Browne. Browne was a friend and physician of Hall, often cited as a leading light in modern science and a man of letters. Browne, like Hall, reflected on ideas in science, philosophy, and psychology that will be seen in building upon a tradition rooted in Augustine, Bernard, Bonaventure, and Calvin. The common denominator in this discussion is the unique and complex way these writers understood the soul, the powers of the imagination, and its relationship to meditation. The way Hall understood the imagination as a faculty of meaning did not come out of vacuum, nor did it reflect modern assumptions arising from a Cartesian worldview.

HALL'S CONTRIBUTION TO AESTHETICAL THEOLOGY

A key figure in seeing the influence of Hall's meditations in subsequent writers of the Puritan imagination is Sir Thomas Browne (1605–82). Browne was a physician in Norwich during the difficult times of civil unrest and became known as a central thinker in medicine, science, and literature. In 1643 he wrote *Religio Medici*, a famous work on meditation, where thoughts on God, nature, and various other topics are presented.[8] In looking at natural science and the book of creation, Browne followed Hall in seeing and affirming the ways nature reflects divine truth. As a scientist in approaching the natural world, Browne was considered to be at the forefront of modern science.[9] Browne saw the tangible world of nature not as something to overcome, but as something to fully sense and look through. Sandra Mayfield describes the connecting threads of thought between the two writers:

---

8. Browne's works continue to be published and studied with great interest. Oxford University Press will soon publish a six-volume series of his works.

9. Kalthoff, "Bohemian Tory and the Oxbridge Knights." This article presents Browne as a pioneer modern scientist who had a mystical approach to his work where his influence from Hall is readily apparent in his use of meditation and the reflection on the natural order.

Both Hall and Browne attempt to describe the capacity of the mind to perceive Divine matter; it is a mysterious and marvelous quality, the gift of God no less than reason. But both Hall and Browne are not willing to lose themselves completely in mystery. Both emphasize the cooperation of reason and faith, or reason and imagination; and both insist that the purpose of meditation is to produce a new ordering of experience, a "new creation" of the mind which arranges the perceptions of the heart and the intellect into meaningful patterns.[10]

Sir Browne was influenced by Hall and, while not a primary concern for source material, this trajectory of the use of imagination is helpful to see that Hall readily had a broad appeal and contemporary relevance when understanding the nature of the soul. How this would influence later writers will be examined more closely in the next chapter. Even with his strong Augustinian theological framework, we see how Hall's occasional meditations were clear examples of his understanding of gaining knowledge from the world of particulars (sensory epistemology). Hall's medieval understanding of the soul allowed for a complexity of variance in how the soul works; this is especially true in the work of mystical theology. Joseph Milosh, reflecting on the English mystics, states, "The beginning of the soul's progress comes with the realization of its own nature."[11]

The sensory faculties of the body reveal the importance of the physical world in human understanding. Human inner urges remind us that the body has a hierarchy of needs; to eat, sleep, etc. The noncorporeal part of the human being, the soul, is not as noticeable or demanding and can be referred to as the "forgotten self." Humans can easily ignore the soul and live as though they don't need to tend to it as much; hence a materialistic worldview of naturalism can be readily affirmed by a purely rational basis.[12]

Hall viewed the soul in a complex manner, but often with language of desire and longing. The Hebrew word for soul is *nephesh*—a living soul—a word that has several meanings, but one concept is captured by the word

10. Mayfield, "Influence of the Art of Mediation," 57.

11. Milosh, *Scale of Perfection*, 89. This is a relevant statement as he considers the role of Hilton's *Scale of Perfection*. He states this importance in understanding the nature of the soul for contemplatives: "It is interesting that a knowledge of the nature of the soul, a knowledge like that one might associate with scholastic theology rather than contemplation, is of great importance to the contemplative; it is also interesting that Hilton's definitions and to a certain extent his terminology of scholastic theology."

12. It can be argued that the roots of naturalism can be traced to Descartes, for reason left to itself presents a certain skepticism that would be found in Hume, who cannot even trust his own sensory perception of reality, let alone affirm a supernatural aspect of truth. See Buckley, *At the Origins of Modern Atheism*.

"longing." Hence, longing and desiring is the *conditio sine qua non* of the human being in the remote corners of the soul, arguably, the *sensis divinitius* left intact, but disabled by original sin. This reflected light, ever yet dim in the heart, is as Hall stated still reflecting a divine imprint: "No visible thing comes so near to the resembling of the nature of the soul, yea, of the God that made it."[13] The essence of being human is not in what can be attained or what can be accomplished but in what the heart has a longing for.[14] Augustine in his work *On the Soul and its Origin* wrote, "The entire nature of man is certainly spirit, soul and body; therefore, whoever would alienate the body from man's nature is unwise."[15] The radical ontological dualism of spirit and body is one of the first heresies of the Christian faith.[16] I refer to this as a "hard dualism" which seeks to distinguish from an imbalanced dualistic philosophy of mind and spirit. The "soft dualism" is a term preferably applied to Bishop Hall and the Augustinian tradition, which rejects and blurs the line between body and soul, or essence and form. This is especially important in relation to speculative meditation, where ontological distinctions between the self and absolute essence, i.e. God, is vitally disregarded. Hall did not embrace a created dichotomy but an incapacitated soul when natural faculties of the soul were damaged in Adam's fall from original righteousness.

In classical thought, Plato imagined the soul to be made up of three parts or faculties.[17] It is of one essence, or, put in another way, the soul is one reality and not something that is attributed to something else. Humans are not bodies with souls, in other words. The soul is simple in its essence, but it is also made up of faculties or powers. "Faculties of the soul" is terminology that both philosophers and theologians like Augustine and later Aquinas used to describe and identify the inner functions, not so much as parts of the soul or distinct areas of a room. From a historical reading of the doctrine of the soul, the consensus of orthodox thought from the patristic period (second century to fourth century) onward understood the soul had three faculties and in similar fashion is exhibited in the thought of Hall. Some would name them differently at times, but they all tended to

---

13. Huntley, *Bishop Joseph Hall*, 134.
14. Hall, *Occasional Meditations*, 31.
15. Augustine, "On the Soul and Its Origin," 5:355.
16. Augustine is addressing the gnostic version of this heresy found in Manicheism. Before that time, Marcion the heretic was excommunicated from the church in AD 144. Part of the reason for his heresy was a radical or "substance dualism," as Corcoran refers to it. See Corcoran, *Rethinking Human Nature*, 13.
17. Angeles, *Dictionary of Philosophy*, 91, states that the three faculties are: a) the appetitive, b) the spirited, and c) the rational.

agree on three.[18] If God is One in Three in the very essence of divine being, then when God created humans in his image, then it makes perfect sense to speak about three-ness, or, as Augustine expressed, a "mirror of the Trinity." Hall reflected this Augustinian viewpoint in stating, "Why may we not say that this soul, as it came from thee, so it is like thee?"[19]

IMAGE OF GOD: THE SOUL'S INTERIOR

Humans are the reflected glory and image bearers of God: the *imago Dei* is imprinted in our created nature by a Triune God who is Father, Son, and Holy Spirit, who is one holy eternal being but forever distinguished in three persons. Human souls as created and contingent beings reflect analogically the essence of the Trinity as one soul with three faculties, which while distinguishable are not separable; the mind (reasonable), the will (volitional), and the emotions (affective). Each of these parts of the soul work together, but they also contain a reflection of God's image in that the mind does not work apart from the will or the emotions and neither do the emotions work apart from the rational part.[20]

Hall affirmed this unity that is a picture of the working cosmos under a Sovereign-ordered nature.

> In the motion of Thine heaven, though some stars have their own peculiar and contrary courses, yet all yield themselves to the sway of the main circumvolution of that First Mover. So, though I have a will of mine own, yet let me give myself over to be ruled and ordered by Thy Spirit in all my ways. Man is a little world: my soul is heaven, my body is earth. If this earth be dull and fixed, yet O God, let my heaven like unto Thine move perpetually, regularly, and in a constant subjection to Thine Holy Ghost.[21]

The mind, while containing the reasonable faculty of the soul, is not simply a thinking part of the soul, as though it controlled the apprehension

---

18. The true debate over the role of the senses and epistemology erupted in the twelfth century. The so called "war of the faculties" at the University of Paris is described in Chang, *Engaging Unbelief*, 102. The Averroes school predominated in the School of Arts, and Aquinas and the old Augustinian school was at the School of Theology.

19. Hall, *Contemplations on the Historical Passages*, 5.

20. Angeles, *Dictionary of Philosophy*, 174. He notes in the theory that the mind is a product of the action of the soul: "The souls as an eternal and immaterial agent acts upon the body and in so doing mental effects are produced such as perceiving, thinking, feeling, willing, imaging, remembering, etc." See also, Jonathan Edwards, *Religious Affections*.

21. Hall, *Occasional Meditations*, 124.

of truth and its logical connections or its cognition. The mind also contains memory, which is more than the storehouse of facts. Using memory in meditation, Hall was not urging a merely a rational process of pulling up files. Rooted in a model of the cosmos that is ordered, connected, and well structured, Hall affirmed that the soul is a small "cosmos." Like the universe, the soul models a way of being, doing, and acting. Owen Barfield in his work *Saving Appearances* stated this central idea: "I hear not with ears alone but with mental habits, memory, imagination, feeling, and will."[22] Jonathan Edwards's analysis of this unity of the soul is described in a similar manner: "Christian or holy practice is spiritual practice . . . but spiritual practice in man is the practice of a spirit and body jointly, or the practice of a spirit animating, commanding, and actuating a body to which it is united and over which it has power given it by the Creator."[23]

THE IMAGINATION: FACULTY OF MEANING

Bishop Hall understood that the imagination is the faculty or disposition of meaning. Memory, in the function of the soul, works with the will and the affective part of the soul to engage the imagination. Imagination is the link between the memory and the affections. It is the creative precognitive shaper of the soul's architecture. The three parts are intellect, will, and emotion. Or, another way to express it is that the soul has a rational part, the thinking part of the soul, sometimes located in the mind and more recently identified with the brain, but that is another modern difficulty that can't be dealt with at this point.[24] The will is the part that deals with rational decisions and human choices. This is where the classic debates between two kinds of philosophies begin their great exploration of what control humans have over their choices. For example, these basic questions illustrate the point: Do we have freedom to choose what we want? Is this freedom to choose always there, or does it have conditions, or is it controlled, dictated by outside forces or energy? Do we live in a universe where we are free, or are things determined, fixed, and ruled by chemicals, a blueprint, or by God? Is there a bit of mixture of the two?[25] These are debatable questions

22. Zaleski and Zaleski, *Fellowship: The Literary Lives of the Inklings*, 473.

23. Edwards, *Religious Affections*, 371.

24. Modern science of neurology and the mind/body problem provide interesting parallels to this discussion. See Kolk, *Body Keeps Score*. Also see Muller's insight into the complexity of post-Reformation views on this topic in his *Divine Will and Human Choice*.

25. Bavinck, *Essays on Religion, Science, and Society*, 199–204. See Bavinck's discussion on the issue of voluntarism and rationalism and his presentation of a view that is

of philosophical and moral theology. What can be affirmed at this point for Hall, especially as it relates to the underlying assumptions of Puritan piety, is the complexity of his understanding of the soul.

For Bishop Hall, the soul is reasonable, and the soul is volitional in a harmonious connection, reflecting the image of God. Human beings think through things and then decide to act and do things based on what they think should be done or what is thought right. Plato and Aristotle used similar concepts of will and reason to describe the powers of the soul. Yet Christian reflection on the soul from an Augustinian viewpoint added the concept of regeneration and the powers of the affections stirred by the agency of the Holy Spirit. Reason and will are important, but the last part the faculty that comes often last in being described is harder to define and isolate, which is affections. To use the word "emotion" is to get an insufficient idea of the old sense of the word. "Affection" in popular and modern minds often is reduced to the corporeal part of human nature because emotions are too closely tied to bodily senses and the physical bodies receiving external information.[26] The word "affection" is a term that includes the emotions but enlarges the concept to the inner aspect of the soul where will and desire connect with the cognitive aspect of being human, resulting in the affective part of the soul. There was in Hall a close connection between the imagination and the affections. Both do not operate apart from reason, but they have a power in shaping knowledge. Jonathan Edwards in his *Religious Affections* described imagination in a succinct manner:

> The imagination is that power of the mind whereby it can have a conception or idea of things of an external or outward nature (that is, of such sort of things as are the objects of the outward senses) when those things are not present and are not perceived by the senses. It is called imagination from the word image; because there by a person can have an image of some external thing in his mind, the thing is not present in reality . . . and the image of them in the mind is very lively.[27]

Edwards showed how at times the imagination can create impressions that seem to be true spiritual illuminations, such as seeing heaven or a vision of Christ on the cross, and these experiences are assumed to be spiritual as though the imagination is an infallible guide. The priority of the affections does not diminish the rational faculty but places the whole of diverse faculties in a complex but unified symphony of parts and notes that

---

more wholistic in approach.

26. Muller, *Dictionary of Latin and Greek Theological Terms*, 19.
27. Edwards, *Religious Affections*, 138–39.

are expressed in deeper longings; underlying chords of the soul's expression in the affections for love of divine communion. As Hall would express it, "God cares not for our phrases, but for our affections."[28]

The imagination is the place where the affections are formed and directed—forming both judgments and desires for beauty. Did Hall express in this vein, a theology of the beatific vision? Is meditation a piety with the telos of union with God? Tom Schwanda states, "Puritans agreed that the transformative nature of seeing God face to face was dynamic and created continued growth in heaven."[29] While the doctrine of deification presents questions in the Western mind regarding essences, in the Eastern tradition it reflects the mystery of union beyond the reredos (a wall concealing the altar) of a veiled human mind longing for God. Dionysius's major work, *Mystical Theology*, presents the beatific vision in this fashion—tasted, but not yet fully possessed.

> Dionysius's model for this intimate vision of God is Moses, who is described as "standing apart from the crowds and [pushing] ahead to the summit [akprotnta] of the divine ascents" (MT1.3, 1000D). The noun Dionysius uses to describe this place of most intimate vision, *akprotes*, literally means "extreme" or "highest." In other words, the experience envisioned by the MT is one in which the creature is permitted to see the highest place than any created being, angel or human, is able to see.[30]

In the Bible, the soul is at times described as a deep well; its depth is beyond our ability to search out and to fully comprehend.[31] But meditation allows us to ponder and to store away experiential truths that are more than facts or external realities. Hall described this deep mystery: "This my soul teaches me of itself, that itself cannot conceive, how capable, how active it is."[32]

Jonathan Edwards called this capability a "new sense."[33] Hall's reliance upon a few key medieval sources for his understanding of the soul in relation

---

28. Hall, *Contemplations on the Historical Passages*, 225.

29. Schwanda, "Saints' Desire and Delight to Be with Christ," 84. Schwanda illustrates from the work of Thomas Watson that it is well within Reformed orthodoxy to affirm this language and understanding.

30. Lashier, "Mediated and Undiluted Light," 61.

31. Ps 69:1: "Save me, O God; for the waters are come in unto my soul." Ps 42:7: "Deep calleth unto deep at the noise of thy waterspouts: all thy waves and thy billows are gone over me."

32. Hall, *Contemplations on the Historical Passages*, 5.

33. Edwards, *Religious Affections*, 133. "And if there be in the soul a new sort of exercises which it is conscious of, which the soul knew nothing of before, and which no improvement, composition, or management of what it was before conscious or sensible

to contemplation is found directly in his work. Frank Huntley affirms, "Hence the sources of Hall's fairly easy-going and pious 'rule of meditation' are Augustine, Bernard and Bonaventure, whom he often invokes as placing their emphasis upon the heart rather than the brain."[34] Understanding these foundational influences, it is necessary for a brief overview of these three sources in how they approached the soul and its faculties, as they are key to a complete picture of medieval contemplative theological praxis.

HALL AND THE CHURCH FATHERS ON THE SOUL

It was Augustine who took the insights of Plato and the biblical framework as an orthodox theologian to bring about a good balance, which is detected in Joseph Hall. "In a number of texts Augustine constructs a ladder of ascent with seven stages of the soul's progress in maturity of comprehension."[35] Augustine viewed the soul, in comparison to the doctrine of the Trinity, in language that is analogical and therefore accessible as a mirror into the inner mystery of being image-bearers of the Creator. Hall was drawing from these Augustinian views as attested by Hambrick-Stowe: "A far broader stream than the Puritan or even the Reformed movement issued from the meditative and mystical tradition of the *Confessions*."[36]

Creativity, as enabled by regenerating grace, therefore, constitutes for Hall the ability to arise in the imaginative role as contemplatives of God's glory. The idea of the Trinity cannot be attained by human reason: "It cannot be discerned or understood by themselves, because the eye of the human mind, being weak, is dazzled in that so transcendent light, unless it be invigorated by the nourishment of the righteousness of faith."[37]

Augustine took from Plato the duality of body and soul, not in a dualistic opposition, as is sometimes characterized by those who argue that

---

could produce, or anything like it; then it follows that the mind has an entirely new kind of perception or sensation, which is in its whole nature different from any former kinds of sensation of the mind, as tasting is diverse from any of the other senses; and something is perceived by a true saint, in the exercise of this new sense of mind in spiritual and divine things, as entirely diverse from anything that is perceived them by natural men, as the sweet taste of honey is diverse from the ideas men get of honey by only looking on and feeling it."

34. Huntley, *Protestant Meditation*, 75.

35. Chadwick, *Augustine*, 52.

36. Hambrick-Stowe, *Practice of Piety*, 27. He also notes, "The tradition was passed to all parties in the seventeenth century through the writings of medieval Catholic mystics, which along with the works of Augustine himself were increasingly available in England."

37. Augustine, "Trinity," III.2.4, 19.

a tint of Manicheism is still left on Augustine's anthropology. Augustine wrote at some length against Neoplatonic heresies by groups influenced by Origen and Plotinus. The negative dualism resulting from this influence is rejected by Augustine. That "hard dualism," in the view of this study, was more of the result of Neoplatonism which came from the influence of Plotinus (205–70).[38]

The soul reflects the Trinity in that it has a mind that both knows and loves, "the mind itself, and the love of it, and the knowledge of it, are three things (*tria quadame*), and these three are one; and when they are perfect they are equal."[39] This idea of a triad that is found throughout creation becomes clearly evident in Augustine. So even in the actions of the soul there is a working together that sets forth an ongoing unity, never one opposed to the other. This is true in the cognitive function of the soul, where understanding is not isolated from the will, but together both provide a web of interaction so that truth is never bare knowledge: "mind, love, knowledge; and this trinity is not confounded together by any commingling."[40] Understanding medieval psychology, while not a central argument in this study, provides a theoretical context for understanding seventeenth-century meditative literature. The medieval model of the soul and its correlative philosophy of knowledge was rooted in a tradition of both Plato and Aristotle's epistemological theories. According to Fredrick Copleston, Plato viewed knowledge coming to the mind in two ways: first through sensory, external experience, and secondly through the property of inner knowledge or innate ideas, which are not related to external data perception of the world. Aristotle built upon the idea of these two sources of knowledge for the mind, but Aristotelians in general, like Aquinas, while not denying "innate knowledge," put a priority on sensory-based knowledge.[41]

There were always varying degrees among scholastic theologians in the direction they moved as either more Platonic or Aristotelian, but the issue related to the medieval spiritual view of the soul affirmed *sapientia* as

38. Chadwick, *Augustine*, 9. The influence of Plotinus and Manicheism is still debated today, but however Augustine is interpreted the realization that his work is heavily noted with biblical references and exegesis must be noted. Among the early church fathers, Origen wrote at length about the soul, but because of his hard dualism of body and soul he would come to some problematic conclusions about the soul. Secondly, Augustine was immensely influenced by the biblical understanding that God created humanity in both body and soul, and that together they reflect the image of God.

39. Augustine, "Trinity," IV.4.4, 127.

40. Augustine, "Trinity," IV.5.8, 128.

41. Copleston, *Medieval Philosophy*, 73–74. In the modern period, this would begin to change under the direction of Rene Descartes, John Locke, and David Hume, who sought to dismiss or distinguish two separate ways of knowing.

experiential truth that illuminates the heart, not in opposition to intellectual knowing through acquisition of truth, but by a mediating reality. Reflecting upon the distinction of knowledge as means of acquired truth (*sapientia* or *scientia*), medieval scholastic theologians affirmed the value of both, and in a sense the two pointed towards the same reality; hence, Augustine suggests, "memory, understanding, will, are not three lives, but one life; nor three minds, but one mind . . . one substance."[42] It is on this trajectory we find Bishop Hall; while he does not always cite sources directly, he did have a clear ability to write from this tradition. "Even among his contemporaries, there were few who combined such density of expression with such amplitude of thought—few who had studied the fathers so diligently, and who could command them so readily."[43]

This is important to see as the next chapter viewed Hall's understanding of the *Beatific Vision*, which he described in his steps of contemplation. Like the three disciples on the Mount of Transfiguration, a spiritual and inner vision of Glory is possible in this life. Augustine hinted at this language: "The Trinity is produced from memory, from *internal vision*, and from the will which unites both."[44] For Augustinian contemplative theology, the aim of true knowledge is for the experience of loving God and seeing him with eyes of faith. So there is a priority given more to spiritual sight than to physical sight or intellectual truth. "For there are two kinds of vision, the one [sensous] reception (*sentientis*), the other of conception (*cogitantis*)."[45] The second is the highest form of knowing, for it is a combination of will/desire and understanding. For Augustine, attaining to the knowledge of God is aimed at the fulfillment of our desires, culminating "in the enjoyment of God," not in an abstract oneness with God.[46]

Nothing strikes at this fulfillment of desires so powerfully as in the often-cited prayer of Augustine in his *Confessions*:

> How late I came to love you, O beauty so ancient and so fresh, how late I came to love you! Unlovely myself, I rushed towards all those lovely things you had made. And always you were with me, and I was not with you . . . You called, you cried, you shattered my deafness. You sparkled, you blazed, you drove away my

---

42. Augustine, "Trinity," XII.11.18, 142.

43. Hall, *Contemplations on the Historical Passages*, xxix.

44. Augustine, "Trinity," III.3.6, 147. "But since the eye of the mind cannot look at all things together, in one glance, which the memory retains, these trinities of thought alternate in a series of withdrawals and successions" (Augustine, "Trinity," VIII.8.151).

45. Augustine, "Trinity," X.9.16.153.

46. Chadwick, *Augustine*, 21.

blindness. You shed your fragrance, and I drew in my breath, and I pant for you. I tasted and I now hunger and thirst. You touched me, and I now burn with longing for your peace.[47]

From Augustine's triads of metaphors and his two ways of seeing and knowing, the priority of the affections is underscored and also affirmed by another source for Hall, and that was Bernard of Clairvaux, a favorite of both medieval contemplatives and Protestant orthodoxy's practical piety. An important feature of affective theology that in Hall challenges the theology of the Tridentine spirituality that the understanding of sensory perception and the priority of faith as an inward illumination by grace. This facet of epistemology is explicit in both Bernard and Bonaventure, as well as defined by John Calvin.

Bernard of Clairvaux (1090–1153)

Bernard of Clairvaux was undoubtedly Hall's most beloved contemplative writer. In his sermon on the Mount of Transfiguration, Bernard was cited multiple times. Hall borrowed the imagery of the mountain to the experience of contemplation. "O Come, let us climb up to the hill, where God sees, or is seen (saith devout Bernard)."[48] Bernard was a pivotal and influential figure in the history of medieval theology and the influence of a reforming monasticism that made profound inroads in both Catholic and Protestant spirituality. As an Augustinian monk, Bernard was known as the founder of the Cistercian order referred to as the Trappist; a tradition that held together strict observance of simple rules of work and prayer but also clear biblical emphasis upon the problem of sin and idolatry. Bernard and his followers put affective theology on the map for a period of increasing corruption in the rise of the late medieval period. It is obvious in the way Hall used bridal metaphors from the Song of Solomon that he drew from the influence of Bernard of Clairvaux. Frank Huntley indicates that Bernard is Hall's favorite "father."[49] Next to Augustine, Bernard stands as the most quoted theologian in *The Art of Meditation*. "The soul is nothing but reason, memory, and will," which is more about the function of the soul than a division of ontology.[50] Preference was for will over intellect in our knowing God. "Bernard nowhere speaks of cooperating grace that comes to the fallen will; only

47. Augustine, *Confessions*, 10.27.
48. Hall, *Contemplations on the Historical Passages*, 513.
49. Huntley, *Bishop Joseph Hall*, 230. There are many places where Hall quotes from Bernard's *Canticles* directly.
50. Tamburello, *Union with Christ*, 23.

to the will already inspired, healed, and empowered by operating grace."[51] This was one reason that Bernard was also an important source for John Calvin. As a Calvinist, Bishop Hall would have been very familiar with the affinity of this strain of piety that fit naturally within the doctrinal matrix of Reformed theology.[52]

The value of affections over the intellect was clear in the writings of Bernard, for in the bridal imagery of the soul's longing, affections were the winecellar where love is delighted.[53]

> For as holy contemplation has two forms of ecstasy, one in the intellect, the other in the will [*in intellectu unus et alter in affectu*]; one of the enlightenment, the other of fervor; one of knowledge, the other of devotion: so a tender affection, a heart glowing with love, the infusion of holy ardor, and the vigor of a spirit filled with zeal, are obviously not acquired from any place other than the wine-cellar.[54]

For Bernard, who was well trained in scholastic theology, true knowledge came from the school of the Holy Spirit teaching the inner heart.

> Knowledge that comes from the school of the Holy Spirit should taste sweeter to me than that of any teacher in any other school . . . So I think that with your hammer you will be able to strike from those rocks something which you would not have carried away from the bookshelves of the teachers by using your sharp wits in study, and that at times you will have sensed something under the shade of trees in the heart of the day that you would never have learned in the schools.[55]

---

51. Tamburello, *Union with Christ*, 31.

52. Tamburello, *Union with Christ*, 57–60. Calvin quotes Bernard from *De Gratia* 6:16: "To will is of nature, but to will aright is of grace" (Reuver, *Sweet Communion*, 33).

53. Reuver, *Sweet Communion*, 46–52. The section on bridal mysticism is a key point to understand the trajectory of this imagery through later Protestants and Puritans. In the view of this study, it is a central concept that unites a broad spectrum of traditions in an orthodox view of mystical experience and union with God. Its biblical paradox protects various forms of imbalance in either a mystical quietism or a split rationalism that leaves affections in an inferior position to reason.

54. Tamborello, *Union with Christ*, 73.

55. Bernard, *Two-Fold Knowledge Readings*, 88.

Bonaventure (1221–74)

Joseph Hall rarely quotes Bonaventure, except in his sermons and polemical work, and always using the revered scholastic theologian in his favor against Rome. "This is the rule of Bonaventure, whom the Romanists honor as a saint, 'This is the part of pious souls, to ascribe nothing to themselves, and everything to the grace of God.'"[56]

Bonaventure was a Franciscan theologian who taught at the University of Paris at the height of an important transition and was a contemporary of Thomas Aquinas. As a disciple of Alexander Hale, he laid stress on the affections as higher than reason in the knowledge of God. The importance of Bonaventure in regard to Hall's work was that he combined his knowledge of Aristotle to complement an Augustinian framework of the soul's faculties. A leading authority on medieval thought, Etienne Gilson, wrote: "When writing the *Commentary*, the Seraphic Doctor uses the Aristotelian term *abstracto* to describe the operation by which the intellect evolves the sensible data of knowledge into the intelligible; but also uses indifferently and exactly in the same sense the Aristotelian expression *abstrahere* and the Augustinian expression *judicare*."[57] So, as Aristotle affirmed the value of sensory knowledge as a way toward the understanding, it was not an avenue open apart from inward sight provided through faith. It is at this point helpful to quote at length how Gilson (who was a leading Thomist scholar) understands Bonaventure:

> Knowledge begins by a perception which implies an initial judgment of the faculty of sensation; it is continued by a judgment of the common sense which characterizes the object as wholesome or harmful; but it is concluded by a third judgment which declares why the sensible perception pleases or displeases us... The impression of beauty, of wholesomeness and pleasure which we experience in perceiving it is explained as soon as the idea of it is formed by us, for it can only cause these impressions in virtue of the proportion of its parts and the proportion of the whole to the organ which perceives it.[58]

---

56. Hall, *Works*, 5:274.

57. Gilson, *Philosophy of St. Bonaventure*, 360.

58. Gilson, *Philosophy of St. Bonaventure*, 361. Bonaventure speaks about eternal principles or spiritual truth which is at the foundation of all knowledge. According to Gilson, this places truth on a firm foundation of objective and experiential understanding that avoids the problems of either mysticism or rationalism. "Thus the immediate activity of the eternal principles is the foundation of all the truth of our knowledge" (Gilson, *Philosophy of St. Bonaventure*, 361).

Secondly, rooted in the Augustinian view of original sin, the fall impairs the *ability* of the human mind to perceive these spiritual realities: "the eternal principles are still accessible, since we do not cease to be men, but they are only partially so . . . because we are deformed by sin."[59] The renewed heart and soul seek to recover the knowledge lost in the fall, hence we see in Bonaventure, as in Augustine, a curvature of the soul towards itself, but upon regeneration the soul it is turned towards desiring God and less for the self.[60] This longing is part of what the soul reflects in seeking a higher knowledge. "Reason then is a condition necessarily required for an appetite to enjoy the faculty of choosing among all the sorts of objects that it is possible to desire."[61] Therefore it is accurate to say *scientia* is necessary towards a right love for God, but it is not determinative, for it needs a *habitus fides* conditioned by the heart. "Like the intellect, the will must be seen first as an innate natural gift, which is determined by an acquired habit."[62]

Habitus would be, according to Bonaventure, this disposition created by faith: "It is a facility in the intellectual and voluntary activity and resembles rather a permanent disposition of the soul than a distinct instrument used by the soul to manifest its activity."[63] Hall followed in this mystical application of scholastic theology that affirmed the imagination not as a separate faculty of the soul, but as a disposition, one that is formed and renewed according to faith. While virtue and the moral life is a consequence of this renewal, it is not its goal. Unlike the school of Stoicism, the ascetic life is not to move towards a transcendent goodness: the *summum bonum*, but towards the love of God, that is the *bonitas Dei*.[64] "To love is to be transformed to the likeness of what one loves, to be conformed to it, to become by an effort of one's whole being another it."[65] Moral transformation is not the goal of contemplation, either in Bonaventure's thought or in the focus here of Hall. Finally, in summary of the soul's faculty and the disposition of the imagination in the renewed soul, Hall followed Augustine, Bernard, and Bonaventure in the view that inward sight, that is, the affective apprehension of divine reality, is with the "eye of faith."

---

59. Gilson, *Philosophy of St. Bonaventure*, 364.

60. Gilson, *Philosophy of St. Bonaventure*, 365. The will for Bonaventure is the "tendency, appetite, or weight: it is essentially an attraction of the soul towards something."

61. Gilson, *Philosophy of St. Bonaventure*, 366.

62. Gilson, *Philosophy of St. Bonaventure*, 379.

63. Gilson, *Philosophy of St. Bonaventure*, 369.

64. Muller, *Dictionary of Latin*, 53.

65. Gilson, *Philosophy of St. Bonaventure*, 393.

This study sets this concept of inward disposition as a decisive distinguishing feature of a meditative theology that shows discontinuity with some strands of the Counter-Reformation, especially in the Jesuit stream of contemplation. In Hall's *Art of Meditation*, the manner of contemplation upon the person and work of Jesus Christ is not with the outward eye and senses, but with the inward perception of faith. In the soul, the contemplations upon Christ's agony, beatings, flowing blood upon the cross is enlarged upon the imagination by faith's perception. This will be further developed and argued in the next chapter, but this inward sense is captured in Hall's words:

> When we would take aim or see most exquisitely, we shut one eye. Thus must we do with the *eyes of the soul*. When we would look most accurately with *the eye of faith*, we must shut the eye of reason, else the visual beams of these two apprehensions will be crossing each other and hinder our clear discerning. Yea, rather let me pull out this right eye [Matt 18:9] of reason that it shall offend me in the interruptions of mine happy visions of God.[66]

Hilton's *Scale of Perfection* also views the eye of faith as a key metaphor in his work and weighs towards the argument that Hall would find in Hilton not only a resource available to him but one that resonated with its theological orientation. This was argued in the previous chapter, but it is necessary to quote at length Hilton's lines to connect the way Hall understood his manner of contemplation as a contribution towards a robust aesthetical imagination that would lay the groundwork for those like Baxter, Browne, Edwards, and even indirectly to Bunyan, Traherne, and the metaphysical poets and the New England Calvinist worldly saints.

> You must know that such gracious intuitions in holy scripture . . . are nothing else but sweet letters, sent between a loving soul and Jesus the beloved; or else, if I am to speak more truthfully, between Jesus the true lover and the souls loved by him . . . St. Paul spoke like this: . . . All that is written for our teaching is written so that by the comfort of scripture we might have hope of salvation. And this is another work of contemplation: to see Jesus in the scriptures after the opening of the spiritual eye. The purer the sight as it gazes, the more comfort is given to the affection as it tastes . . . for the end of the others (knowledge, arts, science) in themselves is only vanity and

---

66. Hall, *Occasional Meditations*, 149.

a passing delight, unless through grace they are turned to this end.⁶⁷

The inward sense of illumination as it has been examined from medieval sources is also a central feature of Reformed epistemology—for apart from the work of the Spirit, fallen minds cannot move toward a fuller knowledge of God. John Calvin's definition of faith supports this concept of inner perception that must come from the work of the Holy Spirit.

> We shall now have a full definition of faith if we say that it is a firm and sure knowledge of the divine favor toward us, founded on the truth of a free promise in Christ, and revealed to our minds, and sealed on our hearts, by the Holy Spirit.⁶⁸

For Calvin, as it was for Hall, knowledge based on our senses—natural reason—is not sufficient for true knowledge of God. In his *Commentary on Romans*, Calvin wrote that among the nations, "there were indeed none who sought not to form some ideas of the majesty of God, and to make him such a God as they could conceive him to be according to their own reason. This presumption I hold is not learned in the schools, but is innate, and comes with us, so to speak, from the womb."⁶⁹

Hence, Calvin affirmed a positive use of the imagination rooted in the fact that there are innate predispositions in the soul/mind where God is at work. As Belden Lane admits,

> Such a God of wondrous majesty filled the Puritan heart with intense anxiety as well as hunger. The soul was driven to introspective meditation and the abandonment of self. It traveled well the valleys of dark despair, as it longed all the while for the splendor of a God beyond its sinful reach. This was a spirituality drawn from the Institutes of Calvin and Luther's commentary on Galatians.⁷⁰

This introspection through the "valley of dark despair" was not a worldly rejection of the creation but ironically and undeniably an affirmation of the external stimuli of God's creation as a help, not a hindrance, for the imagination. Its limitation revealed its utter dependence upon inner light and transcendent grace. It is the dialectic of taste and longing, hiding and being found. Hall's resourcing the trajectory of the medieval mystical

---

67. Hilton, *Scale of Perfection*, 296.
68. Calvin, *Institutes* III.2.7.
69. Calvin, *Commentary on Romans*, 73.
70. Lane, *Landscapes of the Sacred*, 106.

tradition of the soul, even with its scholastic roots, granted him the ability to provide a dialectic of dark and light, knowledge and unknowing, blindness and sight, along a scale of contemplation for the soul to progress in holiness and experience true vision, if only partial, of divine glory—beauty of the Beloved. This is the theological foundation of *The Cloud of Unknowing*, which points to an inner knowledge that moves beyond the intellect. As Hall explains with language echoing this medieval text:

> In vain shall we hope for any revelation from God, but in a cloud. Worldly hearts are in utter darkness; they see not so much as the least glimpse of these divine beams, not a beam of that inaccessible light: the best of his saints see him here, but in a cloud, or in a glass. Happy are we, if God has honoured us with these divine representations of himself; once in his light, we shall see light.[71]

The legacy of this view of the soul, which is argued in the next chapter, is one that was maintained and retooled by Hall for English Protestants of the seventeenth century.

---

71. Hall, *Art*, 522.

Chapter 6

Occasional Meditation and the Puritan Imagination

> What if the man could see Beauty Itself, pure, unalloyed, stripped of mortality and all its pollution, stains, and vanities, unchanging, divine ... the man becoming, in that communion, the friend of God.
>
> —Plato

IN SUMMARY, THERE HAVE been three key directions this study has set forth as the basis for understanding Bishop Hall's role as a foundational author and shaper of a "Reformed mysticism."[1] Looking primarily at Hall's *Art of Divine Meditation*, it can be argued that this example of Protestant contemplative practice had bearing on subsequent thought and spirituality among Reformed expressions of piety. First, as a loyal churchman, Hall had the

---

1. Oberman, *Harvest of Medieval Theology*, 327, 331. Note that often nominalism and mysticism are "supposedly mutually exclusive" (Oberman, *Harvest of Medieval Theology*, 328). This is not the case, and the medieval tradition that the Puritans drew upon held these streams together. According to Aquinas, mysticism is the contemplation of the vision of God, which was truth. The definition of mysticism by Jean Gerson is one readily affirmed by seventeenth-century Protestants: "[Mysticism is a reaching] of the soul to a union with God through the desire of love, which resides not in the intellectual, but in the affective power of the soul, and has not the *verum* but the *bonum* as its object" (Oberman, *Harvest of Medieval Theology*, 328). These are critical assessments by Oberman, which this study affirms as needed and more nuanced for claiming the validity of Reformed mysticism.

support of the royal court, and, as a moderate, he was positioned to write and commend a practical piety that reflected the theology of the English Prayer Book and the canons of the established church.² Yet, as a representative of the Synod of Dordt and defender of its assertions, Hall had the respect of a broad base of Calvinists and Puritans.³ Secondly, in his use of source material, Hall did not merely offer an alternative to Counter-Reformation piety that was coming from Continental mystics. He drew from a wider spectrum of medieval traditions in continuity with patristic theology and ascetic practice.⁴ Jean Leclerq makes this lucid and insightful statement: "The monastic Middle Ages is essentially patristic because it is thoroughly penetrated by ancient sources and, under their influence, centered on the great realities which are at the very heart of Christianity and give its life."⁵ Chapter 4 addressed the similar styles and thoughts of Walter Hilton and other English medieval mystics with the work of patristic writers of the Eastern tradition. By a careful analysis of Hall's *Art of Meditation* and his other works of contemplative theology throughout his life, that chapter demonstrated that Leclercq's assertion is valid. Even the work of Mauburnus in Paris was a collection of contemplative materials brought together for the reforming of his monastery. "At the end of his life, Mauburnus became an abbot at the monastery of Livry near Paris, one of the monasteries he had reformed according to the precepts of the *devotio moderna*. *The Rosetum*, his most important work, is an extensive introduction to the practice of meditation."⁶

---

2. Thornton, "The Caroline Divines," 435. Thornton notes the connection between Anglican spirituality and the influence of the Prayer Book: "Study of the Prayer Book, as ascetical system as well as liturgical composition, is central to the study of Caroline spirituality. The two are indissociable."

3. Huntley, *Bishop Joseph Hall*, 67. Huntley reflects on the way Hall expressed a *via media*, in the tumultuous period before the civil war: "His desire to protect the *via media* from the two extremes that threatened it: one argument directed against Roman Catholics, and the other against the 'separating Brownists' . . . it was not until Joseph Hall travelled to the Low Countries with Sir Edmund Bacon that he began to argue in writing against one church from which his own had 'reformed' and another which was trying he felt, to 'reform' him. 'How senseless are these two extremes', he cried; 'of the papists, that one man hath the keys; of the Brownists, that every man hath them!'"

4. Thornton, "Caroline Divines," 432. Speaking of the Caroline Age, Thornton notes that the spiritual flowering of the period is "traceable to the New Testament and the Fathers. So, in order to understand and evaluate the spirituality of the Caroline age it must be seen as a strand in a continuing tradition . . . Some acquaintance with the English fourteenth-century writers is an essential prologue to Caroline studies." This undergirds the source theory of this study, which highlights the fourteenth-century English mystics as key sources for Hall as well as Eastern writers.

5. Leclercq, *Love of Learning*, 107.

6. Hasche-Burger, "Music and Meditation," 348.

This study builds upon the work of Frank Huntley, whose view that Hall drew from a wider source material, especially from other medieval writers than previously thought, gives substance to the view that Bishop Hall was not a minor author but a positive and enduring shaper of a Protestant view of meditation and the imagination.[7] This positive function of the soul's faculty of meaning is a central feature of Hall's method and understanding of meditation, which is at the heart of this study.

Finally, the way Hall understood the soul and its faculties within the framework of medieval scholastic thought sets him apart as a distinct example of using the imagination in a positive and creative way that lays the groundwork for a robust application of aesthetics in theology. This chapter explores the role of the imagination as viewed by Hall, his sources and the historical context of the seventeenth century, revealing the continuity his view had with medieval and patristic monastic thought. It also provides the impetus to applying his insights to the wider subject of Reformed aesthetics.

ASSESSING HALL'S LEGACY

The spiritual practice of meditation, often likened to climbing a mountain, requires faithful guides. This study has sought to recover the pivotal and foundational role that Bishop Hall had both on Puritan piety and the shaping of a distinctly Calvinist imagination. It is no less true today than when in the mid-nineteenth century Huntington Clapp of Andover Seminary lamented the paucity of sources related to Hall for an American readership.[8] Hall's works are very limited in scope and relatively inaccessible for today's audience. As stated previously, this chapter seeks to underline the need to reclaim Hall's approach to meditation as a supreme and critical application of medieval Augustinian mysticism that addresses ongoing theological issues related to spiritual practices and furthermore yields a theology of aesthetics that affirms a positive view of the imagination for the Calvinist tradition.[9] The trajectory of how Hall utilized the imagination within a

---

7. Hambrick-Stowe, *Practice of Piety*, 38. Louis Martz was mistaken, therefore, when he argued that Puritans began to engage in systematic meditation only after Richard Baxter published *Saint's Rest*. According to Martz, Puritans generally denounced devotional methods as mere human invention.

8. Hall, *Selection from the Writings of Joseph Hall*, vi. "It is an evil sign of the times, that while our Christian libraries are flooded with weak dilutions of religion-made-easy, no American edition of the works of this sterling author has ever been issued and the only specimen of his writings to be obtained in this country, is a mangled copy of some of his 'Contemplations.'"

9. Hambrick-Stowe, *Practice of Piety*, 38. "Horton Davies followed Martz when

faculty of the soul both exhibited and enriched a broad spectrum of affective theology within a natural revelation under the influence of divine illumination. Hence, this approach to meditation is not mysticism unfettered. Yet it is not merely reason aided by revelation. The canvas in which the vision of Christ's glory and the truths of God's word is laid over is more than just the rational mind but stretches over the entire essence of the soul. Hall's *Art* is not only a call to believe that God is good and lovely, but to see and "taste the goodness of the Lord."[10]

A REFORMED RELUCTANCE

Beauty, if not well disciplined, proves not a friend, but a traitor.[11]

The Westminster Assembly divines shared a strong view that any kind of representation of God in worship was against the Bible and a form of idolatry. This concern about the tendency and proclivity of the "idol faculty" to make false gods and to diminish the glory of God's nature was central among Reformed theologians even though the role of the imagination was varied. The *Westminster Larger Catechism* (WLC) states that the prohibition against any images or representations of anything in heaven also applies to "inward images."[12] Calvin wrote about the distortion of God's natural revelation by a fallen human nature that rather than follow God's abundant signs in nature and the human body suppress truth. Since Calvin does not dismiss natural revelation but affirms it, the WLC needs to be seen in light of a corruption of original goodness in human faculties. Hence, it is not inward imagining that is wrong, but a sinful and distorted imagining.

The question then revolves around the meaning of images in the mind and begs many queries: Does this prohibit the use of the imagination when contemplating God, or the person and work of Christ? How is it possible to not imagine when reading Scripture, or is this a feature of human fallenness that is always broken and sinful? Hence, there is a tilt towards a negative use

---

he emphasized Baxter's uniqueness in using the composition of place methodology. 'Employing the senses,' Davies stated, was 'usually regarded as inimical by Protestants to true spirituality.' Even U. Milo Kaufmann, who pushed back the use of 'sensual' and affective' methods to Richard Sibbes, retained Martz's framework by presenting Puritan homiletical method as bound to a 'literal hermeneutics' that excluded sense and imagination" (Hambrick-Stowe, *Practice of Piety*, 38).

10. In Psalm 34:8, we see the experience of knowing God is a higher level of knowledge than just the intellectual knowing.

11. Hall, *Contemplations on the Historical Passages*, 227.

12. Westminster Larger Catechism, *Question 109*, in Calvin, *Institutes* I.5.4.

of the imagination broadly speaking: the "vain imagination" would be the realm of the dark space of "fantasy" and sinful distortions to be repented from and restricted from use. Or is there a Reformed alternative, a positive role where the redeemed imagination that is informed by the Bible and shaped by its truth so that it becomes a guide towards a "further beauty" that is not in violation of the second commandment? David Davis argues that under the influence of Peter Martyr Vergmili and Theodore Beza, the English Reformation took a more nuanced view of the role of certain types of images and the cultivation of art.[13]

Hall, as a Calvinist and a Conformist, may be an example of moderation when it comes to the broad question of the appropriate use of art, but his thinking about a positive role of a redeemed imagination is also affirmed by Puritans such as Thomas Watson, Richard Baxter, and Jonathan Edwards.[14] The view that the imagination is both broken but enabled by regenerating grace to be a useful and important realm for spiritual growth is detailed in this chapter.

Thomas Aquinas was often supported by the nominalism of the intellectual emphasis of later medieval scholasticism, but his statement here reveals a deeper appreciation of the imagination: "Therefore it is clear that for the intellect to understand actually, not only when it acquires new knowledge, but also when it uses knowledge already acquired, there is need for the act of the imagination."[15] As the conscience was previously conceived as the organ of morality, the imagination is not so much as a faculty of the soul, but a function, or place of meaning.[16] Imagination is for Hall the *habitus* where

---

13. Davis, *Seeing Faith, Printing Pictures*, 55, 57. "Theodore Beza held a more sympathetic position on the meditative function of images ... Popular in Reformation England for his catechetical writings and the commentary notes in the Geneva Bible, Beza was also known for his approval of illustrations. Echoing John Fox's opinion on printed images, Beza ... seemed to think that printed images were an altogether different category of visual representation, one that could be very beneficial. In his *Icones* and elsewhere, Beza promoted poetic and aesthetic expressions of faith as supplements to the preaching and reading of the Word." His book argues the great influence of Peter Martyr Vermigli in England: "His theology is often more nuanced and subtle, like that of Philip Melanchthon, lacking the reactionary sentiments of someone on the front lines of religious conflict."

14. Hambrick-Stowe, *Practice of Piety*, 159.

15. Aquinas, *Summa contra Gentiles*, 1.8.1, 76.

16. Lewis, "Bluspels and Flanlansferes," 10–11. The way Hall understands the role of imagination is similar in thought as expressed by Lewis as an organ of meaning, but Hall does not say this explicitly. The word used by Hall is "conscience" or "the heart," but he has in mind a deeper understanding of the faculty where metaphors are formed or, as argued previously, the precognition of truth. See this view in Lewis: "But it must not be supposed that I am in any sense putting forward the imagination as the organ

truth is fully looked through and along with to a deep reality. "O Thou who are the true light, shine ever through all the blind corners of my soul; and from these weak glimmerings of grace bring me to the perfect brightness of Thy Glory."[17]

THE BROKEN IMAGINATION

Thomas Watson's treatise on meditation is remarkably similar to Hall's work in that it incorporates both a form and a freedom to the practice. He also includes a chapter on occasional meditation, highlighting the importance and role of using metaphors in thinking about God. Thomas Watson was also a mainstream Puritan in his cautionary stance towards idolatry, in the sense that he maintained a strong suspicion of the danger that the imagination presents.

> There is a strange utopia in the imagination of some men; they take those for true principles that are false; and if they err in their principles, they must be wrong in their meditations. Thus the mind, having laid in wrong principles, the meditation must be erroneous, and a man at last goes to hell upon a mistake! Therefore be sure you read before you meditate, so that you may say, "It is written!"[18]

So, the danger maintained by Watson is countered by the importance of reading Scripture prior to meditation, since God's truth needs to be the barometer of understanding divine reality and not erroneous impulses. There is a legitimate point to make that following this rule of Watson can itself become unreliable if the focus is merely outward and perfunctory rather than attended with true affections. Hall and Watson note the practice of Jesuits begin with Scriptures and rely upon certain passages to begin their meditation. One could argue that Ignatian spirituality is biblically-based in a literal sense of using a text of Scripture; however, Hall was concerned with reducing all truths, even Scripture, to bare and external propositions alone. The problem of idolatry is not merely limited to the imagination but can also become a concern relating to intellectual propositions.

---

of truth. We are not talking of truth, but of meaning: meaning which is the antecedent condition both of truth and falsehood, whose antithesis is not error but nonsense. I am a rationalist. For me, reason is the natural organ of truth; but imagination is the organ of meaning. Imagination, producing new metaphors or revivifying old, is not the cause of truth, but its condition."

17. Hall, *Occasional Meditations*, 134.
18. Watson, *Christian on the Mount*, 98.

In noting the caution of Jonathan Edwards against reading and thinking on bare truths and false affections, the Scriptures can be used to a false understanding of God. "Take away all the moral beauty and sweetness of the Word, and the Bible is left wholly a dead letter, a dry, lifeless, tasteless thing."[19] Peter Toon is right to see that imagination cut off from divine assistance is always problematic: "In fact Protestant teaching affirms that sin has not only affected the whole mind, giving it a basis towards the rejecting of God as the Lord God, but also (via the devil's temptations) can run riot in the imagination (which is naturally wild and free) causing it to make evil images, and creating sinful desires."[20]

The Irish bishop and friend of Hall, James Ussher, is representative of a dual focus in approaching imagination. His credentials as a Calvinist are unquestioned, but his reluctance in the use of images and art for worship is not merely an iconoclastic spirit of times. It reflected a biblically rich and spiritual awareness of a deeper beauty than a regenerate mind can contemplate. This positive claim and role of the imagination is seen here in his *Body of Divinity*:

> To represent him by any shape, is most of all forbidden and condemned. For it is a great sin to conceive or imagine in our hearts, that he is like anything, how excellent soever we think it, (Acts 17:29) but it is much worse so to set him out to the view of others, considering that the Mind can conceive a further Beauty than the hand of the Artificer can express.[21]

The final statement of Ussher's implicit understanding of the role of the imagination is that set free from the ravages of sin, a regenerated mind can do far more and express greater beauty of divine truth than can be expressed merely relying on the imagination of others.[22] This, in a sense, puts

---

19. Edwards, *Religious Affections*, 200.

20. Toon, *Meditating as a Christian*, 119–21. Toon points out the fact that the Bible uses the term "vain imaginations" in a specific sense, not condemning all imagination. "Having said this we must also note that the world for the cogitations of unregenerate sinners (as in AV/KJV and the book by William Perkins, *Treatise of Man's Imagination*, 1600) and as the technical term in faculty psychology for the power of the mind to make images. The two have often been confused and this has not helped the cause of those who wanted to give a positive role to the imagination." As an Anglican with a strong Reformed theology, Toon represents the kind of model that is found in Hall that is cautionary but positive towards art, imagination, and its spiritual use.

21. Ussher, *Body of Divinity*, 307. Ussher also wrote a book on meditation that came several years later than Hall's work and is indebted to Hall's approach; see Ussher, *Method for Meditation*.

22. Ussher, *Body of Divinity*, 129. Ussher states there are five faculties of the soul: the understanding, the memory, the will, the affections, and the conscience.

an individual in the role of seeking the further beauty of God's truth rather than as a secondary receiver filtered through fallen lenses. This "new sense," as Edwards would describe it, is a positive assertion that imagination is not restricted by a commonly conceived narrow Puritan view of the soul but is set forth in its intended creative role.[23] This incentive for creativity that is a feature of Hall's method and understanding of imagination in meditation is the heart of the thesis set forth in this study. Although indebted to Martz's original insights into Hall's contribution of a Protestant meditation, this study believes Martz (as well as Kaufmann) places Hall in a restrictive and more intellectual line of tradition.[24] This is also disputed by Joel Beeke and Mark Jones in their review of the role meditation had for the Puritans.[25] This study follows that central criticism; in establishing the evidence that Martz and Kaufmann were not seeing the full picture of the philosophical differences between Protestant piety and Ignatian spirituality. Frank Huntley did much to correct the bias and gaps of historical research, but these writers where primarily concerned with the discussion in a literary context. Hence, in this research, the historical theological underpinnings provide more lenses in which to properly access the totality of Hall's approach and influence. In summary, Hall stood in the lineage of Bernard, Bonaventure, and Gerson, to name a few, that put an emphasis on the volitional part of the soul, hence including the affective knowledge as on equal footing as

23. Kaufmann, *Pilgrim's Progress*, 126. Then he asks, "Why did not the Puritan put the imagination into harness and tame it by using it? The answer is implicit in the Puritan orientation toward logos." So he concludes because Protestants sought an "unambiguous authority." So when it came to meditation, to the Puritan the "imagination was not so much feeble instrument to be sanctified and used despite its weakness as an utter irrelevancy. The Puritan was not likely to meditate upon events in the life of Christ but rather upon doctrines or specific propositions of Scripture."

24. Kaufmann, *Pilgrim's Progress*, 124. He also follows Martz in placing Hall as a restrictive, intellectualist model of meditation. In the "orderly and logical" writing of Hall, "[meditation] is carefully reined in and controlled by the reason, and the suspect imagination is granted no opportunity to introduce a contraband intuition that might transcend logical categories" which "owed more to a positive emphasis which displaced the use of the imagination, that to the simple working out of the prejudice against that faculty is argued by the fact that Catholicism and Puritanism did not differ in the basic evaluation of the imagination, though Catholic devotion employed the faculty in meditation."

25. Beeke and Jones, *Puritan Theology*, 892. This article describes Kaufmann's theory that places Hall and Ambrose on a restrictive line that reduces meditation to merely reflection on Scripture, hence a cognitive function. "Moreover, Kaufmann's assessment of Hall and Ambrose fails to take into account the remarkable freedom that both writers gave to scriptural imagination and use of the senses." Indeed, this thesis is in full agreement in the present study and can firmly commend the statement, "the Puritans serve as mentors on how we can use sanctified imagination."

cognitive knowledge. The two belong together, even though, sequentially ordered, cognitive truth begins first. Like the scale of a mountain, a climber begins not at the summit but at the base. Peter Toon encapsulates the twin focus in a succinct way: "Meditation is a reasoned application of the mind to some supernatural truth in order to penetrate its meaning, love it and carry it into practice with the assistance of divine grace."[26] Climbing the summit was not a leap in the dark, suspending reason, but an ascent from reason to the affections, transcending the limits of bare cognitive knowledge to a deeper experience of divine truth.

BISHOP HALL AND THE EVOCATION OF NATURE

In a time when Foxe's *Book of Martyrs* inflamed the imagination of Protestant England with the mystic of persecution, it is often forgotten that after the Marian persecutions others suffered for their faith. Hall went to prison for his loyalty to the crown and Bunyan for his Nonconformity. Indeed, it was a time of political changes for everyone. It would be difficult to understand Bunyan and the enduring appeal of his work apart from Hall's influence on the meditative tradition. The pilgrim in Bunyan's signature work began his journey by meditating.[27] There is common ground in approaches and to the reality that both Hall and Bunyan were persecuted for their views, however different they stood in ecclesiology.[28] Joseph Hall, like Bunyan, spent many cold nights imprisoned for his views. However, Hall was confined by Parliament in the Tower of London for his views on conformity in ecclesiology. Indeed, it was not only the Nonconforming separatists that suffered persecution and loss during the English Civil Wars. Seven years before Hall was elected bishop of Exeter and placed in the Tower for six months, he wrote an occasional meditation inspired by watching coals catch fire in a hearth. No doubt thinking on the coming conflict within his land, he wrote:

> When we see the Church on a flame, it is too late to complain
> of the flint and the steel . . . But why should not peace and truth

26. Toon, *Meditating as a Christian*, 182.

27. Kaufmann, *Pilgrim's Progress*, "The readers's first glimpse of Christian finds him in anguished meditation, standing in a field, with a book in his hand. The scene happily dramatizes a notable motif of Puritan discussions of meditation."

28. Bouyer, *History of Christian Spirituality*, 160. There is a bias evident in Bouyer regarding Bunyan, but he does see a line of influence from Hall to him. "It is a sort of instinctive and simplified equivalent of the systems of meditation worked out by Hall and Baxter. But Bunyan's analysis of the heart and its hidden springs took the form of a sort of animated Epinal print and as such has charmed generation after generations (or else bored it to tears!)."

be as successful in dilating itself to the gaining of many hearts? Certainly, these are in themselves more winning if our corruption had not made us indisposed to good. Oh God, out of an holy envy and emulation at the speed of evil, I shall labor to enkindle others with these heavenly flames. It shall not be my fault if they spread not.[29]

This example of meditation points to the wider issue of how Hall applied the imagination in the service of godly contemplation. It was his life's work to direct his writing to cultivate devotion to Christ, which was the greater need in England than to win the battle of ecclesiastical Conformity. In the question of epistemology, his work on meditation conveys how Hall could appropriate sensory knowledge of sight, sound, and tactile experience to contemplate on divine truth. This openness to creativity in the imagination sets forth the thesis of how Hall provides a foundation for a Protestant mysticism unique and influential for later writers.

SENSORY-BASED KNOWING

The early part of the *Art* showed Hall understanding that meditation on the book of nature was an important and profitable exercise for Christians. While this appears in his book on rules for a different type of meditation, one more deliberate and intentional, it came early to reveal Hall's understanding that this is not a minor or unnecessary feature of spiritual piety. He stated it is rather harmful to neglect it, and doing so dishonors God who created the world as a showcase of his glory.

This world-embracing realism is not a platonic escape to the world of the spiritual and the ethereal form.[30] There is also a naturalness to this kind of meditation in that it only requires a *habitas* or sense of being to the presence and revelation of God at all times. This type has no rule, for it will "vary . . . according to the infinite multitude of objects."[31] Open to the natural order of the world and the serendipitous nature of life, "man is placed in this stage of the world, to view the several natures and actions of the creatures." The human heart does not need to shut out the natural world to contemplate on ultimate truth or divine reality. Augustine strongly identifies two ways of seeing and knowing: there is inward illumination and sensory

---

29. Hall, *Art*, 138.

30. Hall would reject the kind of dualism which results more from Neoplatonic thoughts found in the speculative mysticism that rejects the world of matter and body for the spiritual.

31. Hall, *Art*, 49.

cognitive knowledge. Regarding the influences of the senses in thinking, he states: "The will occupied by thoughts turns away from the senses, and so informs the eye of the mind (*acies*) by various images of sensible things, as though those sensible things were actually perceived."[32] Following the notion that nature is a book where God is making known his glory, Hall echoes the words of John Calvin: "The world is a stage where God's glory is displayed."[33] This affirmation of nature as a legitimate and even revelatory aspect of experiencing truths of God is seen in Herman Bavinck: "The notion that God works only and exclusively in the human heart and has everywhere retreated from his creation is simply untenable."[34]

Theologians who followed this notion would agree with the view of Jonathan Edwards, whose example of occasional meditation was the basis of many pages of writings on the natural world. In his *Observations*, Edwards notes:

> We have shown that the Son of God created the world for this very end, to communicate Himself in an image of his own excellency... So that, when we are delighted with flowery meadows and gentle breezes of wind, we may consider that we see only the emanations of the sweet benevolence of Jesus Christ. When we behold the fragrant rose and lily, we see his love and purity. So the green trees and fields, and singing of birds, are the emanations of His infinite joy and benignity. The easiness and naturalness of trees and vines are shadows of his beauty and loveliness. The crystal rivers and murmuring streams are the footsteps of His favor, grace and beauty.[35]

Indeed, one can say that Hall's spirituality embraced the doctrine of creation in a way that directed practical piety toward nature and to God rather than to God by overcoming nature. "God made all these for man, and man for his use..."[36] Accordingly, if we fail to ponder the work of God—his

---

32. Augustine, "Trinity," XI.4.7.148.

33. Calvin, *Commentary on Romans*, 70. This is a term that Calvin uses several times in his works, affirming the value of natural revelation to those who are open to see.

34. Bavinck, *Reformed Dogmatics*, 1:75.

35. Lane, *Landscapes of the Sacred*, 104–08. Lane represents a view of spirituality that is at times pluralistic, but he understands the balance of Edwards. "Edwards wrote immeasurably more about the excellence of God's beauty than he ever dealt on the horror of divine omnipotence. The capacity of humans to grasp, by an aesthetic (almost sixth) sense of the heart, the very glory of God would form the height of Puritan devotion at its best" (Lane, *Landscapes of the Sacred*, 104).

36. Huntley, *Bishop Joseph Hall*, 73.

truth in his creatures—then we fail to use them as God intended. The book of nature is meant to be utilized for deeper truth.

There are many instances in the Scriptures where occasional meditation and the use of nature is found. Hall looked to Solomon who "put the sluggard to school unto the ant."[37] Or where Jesus "sendeth the distrustful to the lily of the field."[38] Hall alluded to Psalm 8 when he wrote, "view of the glorious frame of the heavens, was led to wonder at the merciful respect God hath to so poor a creature as man."[39] Outside of the biblical testimony is found others like Augustine who saw in the brook near his home the ordered structure of music and the design of God's creation. Hence, there are manifold reasons for this spiritual practice that engages the senses in a world-affirming and useful employment of the natural world. "The creatures are half lost, if we only employ them, not learn something of them," whether it is a morning songbird or a horse that pulls a wagon.[40] The natural world and animals are not merely created for utilitarian purposes but exhibit spiritual value for the truths that they embody in a universe bursting forth in the sound of the Creator's glory (Psalm 8). The rich tradition of Calvinism with its affirmation of the book of nature undergirds the positive view of nature's ability to reflect and reveal the Creator's glory, if eyes of faith are open to see: "if we read this great volume of the creatures, and take out no lesson for our instruction."[41]

There can be a concern that nature and human proclivity to distort provides a reason to be cautious if not reluctant to use this method of meditation. The danger is to move towards an Emersonian naturalism that can easily dispense with transcendence and the importance of revealed truth in Scripture. Hall did waive caution, but the hazard for him was not so much in the abuse or distortion as its neglect or careless exercise, or to use the image of the traveler: merely an accidental tourist flying through the experience of nature's voice. Here we find that there are certain pitfalls in the employment of the imagination, even when reflecting on the book of nature. The use of the imagination can be distorted and twisted by sin, as Hall stated, where "our meditations degenerate, and grow rather perilous to the soul."[42] But the danger resides more in an overfamiliarity, using the same meditation over and over, becoming too rote and predictable and not learning new truths of

---

37. Huntley, *Bishop Joseph Hall*, 73.
38. Huntley, *Bishop Joseph Hall*, 73.
39. Huntley, *Bishop Joseph Hall*, 73.
40. Hall, *Art*, 49.
41. Hall, *Art*, 49.
42. Hall, *Art*, 50.

God's world: "Having given us the scope of the whole world; so that there is no creature, event, action, speech, which may not afford us new matter of meditation. As travelers in a foreign country make every sight a lesson, so ought we in this pilgrimage."[43] Lane asks a pertinent question: "How can one develop a legitimate theology of place-being able to recognize once again the Shekinah glory of a God we thought altogether driven from the world? And how is this done without resorting to a syrupy nature mysticism which dissolves all boundaries between God, the world, and our human response?"[44] It is a question that reflects deeply on the issue of "worldly saints" who can see the world as a vessel of grace rather than an obstacle to it. By using the term "extemporaneous meditations," the emphasis moved towards a freshness and openness to the senses. Here the warning about the imagination appeared to be a concern of not engaging it enough in application to the external world. The restriction is more of the careless and mindless person who implements the task of meditation without intentional mindfulness and engagement of the whole being with the world around us.

Hall ended with this stern admonition to careless travelers: "Hast thou so long read these capital letters of God's great book,[45] and canst thou not yet spell one word of them? The brute creatures see the same things with clear, perhaps better eyes: if thine inward eyes see not their use, as well as thy bodily eyes their shape, I know not where is more reasonable or less brutish."[46] Is it reason, the ability to rationalize, that separates humanity from animals? Hall seems to extol the virtue of the natural world, if humanity fails to heed to the truth of God found in God's creation (Rom 1). Writing in 1746, a century later, Jonathan Edwards extolled the virtue and importance of the inner eye of faith and how there is a danger to trusting the affections and false imaginations, yet true faith is not capable without it.

> [God] best knows our nature; He knows the nature and manner of His own operations; He best knows the way of our safety; he knows what allowances to make for different states of His church, and different tempers of particular persons, and varieties in the manner of His own operations, how far nature may resemble grace, and how far nature may be mixed with grace,

---

43. Lane, *Landscapes of the Sacred*, 19.

44. Lane, *Landscapes of the Sacred*, 19.

45. Hall understands nature as one of the three books of God. The Dutch theologian Bavinck clarifies the same point in his *Reformed Dogmatics*, 2:425: "The whole world is thus the realization of an idea of God; a book containing letters, large and small, from which his wisdom can be known."

46. Hall, *Art*, 50.

what affections may rise from imagination, and how far imagination may be missed with spiritual illumination.[47]

True to this caution is the realization that false affections and false imaginations can be deceptive and give the illusion of reality. Counterfeit truths point to the fact that there is truth behind them. Among English writers who, like Hall, affirmed a positive role of the imagination was Richard Sibbes. It was in the "affectionate piety"[48] of Sibbes where it is affirmed that the sacraments, pictures of the visible signs, were meant to engage the imagination. "What is the use of the Sacraments, but to help our souls by our senses, and our faith by imagination; as the soul receives much hurt from imagination, so it may have much good thereby."[49] Faith without imagination and the cultivation of meaning in the soul leads to a dead and empty faith, devoid of reality. Hall reaffirmed the powers of the soul, mind, and heart as the fullest expression of biblical faith.

CONCLUSION

If someone proved to me that Christ is outside truth, and that in reality, the truth was outside Christ, then I would prefer to remain with Christ rather than with the truth.

—*Fyodor Dostoevsky*[50]

This study is indebted to the scholarship and literary work of Frank Huntley. His theory that Hall represents a positive contribution to the role of the imagination and his broadening the source material to include writers like Thomas a Kempis provide the incentive to delve deeper in the extent of the tradition that Hall would explore. Furthermore, beyond the wide use of sources, Huntley had a clear sense of connecting Hall to other poets and

---

47. Edwards, *Religious Affections*, 381–82. Edwards gives an extensive treatment on the role of the affections in knowledge, and he reveals a deep understanding, similar to Hall on the way sensory input is used in the imagination. There might be even an allusion to types of meditation that are made too routine and restrictive to the imagination, perhaps a reference to Jesuit models: "It would tend to deliver us from innumerable perplexities, arising from the various inconsistent schemes there are about methods and steps of experience. It would greatly tend to prevent professors neglecting strictness of life and tend to promote their engageness and earnestness in the Christian walk."

48. Dever, *Affectionate Theology of Richard Sibbes*.

49. Sibbes, *Soul's Conflict*, 114.

50. Frank, *Dostoevsky: The Mantel of Prophet*, 712. Written in a letter while he was in a Siberian prison camp in 1854.

writers that are influenced in the line of Hall but not often recognized by other scholars. "Vaughan, Herbert, Traherne, Donne and Jonson and Herrick in their religious poems—all English, Protestant, ejaculatory, emblematic and meditative poets—may very well have been influenced, directly or indirectly, not by St. Ignatius of Loyola, but by the art and practice of the Anglican Puritan Joseph Hall."[51] Hall is mentioned as an influence in a wide spectrum of later spiritual writers, from Edwards and Spurgeon to orthodox theologians. Sergei Hackel notes that Hall's work was influential in that of the Russian bishop and mystic St. Tikhon of Zadonsk (1724–83).[52]

The classification of Hall as an ecumenical Calvinist, as previously asserted, or the label of Reformed contemplative (or even mystic), is underscored by the legacy that Hall left in the formation of an enduring ascetical theology that flowered the imagination without restricting it. Furthermore, it is not the republication of his *Art of Divine Meditation*, as is true in the traditions of Ignatian or Salesian spirituality, that judges the legacy of Hall, but the model of a meditation that revitalized a robust medieval and patristic balance of mind, heart, and active life as well as ascetic piety that is traced broadly in the works of a "great cloud of witnesses" (Heb 12:1). Works of occasional meditations nurtured from engagement with the world proliferated in the eighteenth century, such as Hervey's *Meditations and Contemplations*.[53] In the nineteenth century, Hall finds expression; a strangely different cultural expression in the Russian Orthodoxy of Dostoevsky's novels. Joseph Frank, a literary scholar, writes: "The influence of Saint Tikhon Zadonsky, a mid-eighteenth-century Russian monk elevated to sainthood in 1860, goes back a long way in Dostoevsky's moral-spiritual evolution."[54] The character Father Zosima is modeled after St. Tikhon, whose approach of worldly ascetic piety was influenced by Hall and the German pietism of Lutheranism.[55] It is in the *Brothers Karamazov* where Father Zosima recounts

---

51. Huntley, *Bishop Joseph Hall*, 101.

52. Hackel, "Russian," 268. "The influences of German pietism (in the person of Joseph Arndt) and of evangelical Anglicanism (Joseph Hall) are to be traced in his writings: these are curiously evangelical (and somewhat emotional) in tone, while yet Orthodox in substance." He is also referred to as Bishop Tikhon or Tikhon Zadonsky.

53. Hervey, *Meditations and Contemplations*, 1:279. He names Hall as a theological influence, and his work was dismissed by John Wesley as too Calvinistic.

54. Frank, *Dostoevsky: The Mantel of Prophet*, 454. "He may well have come across Saint Tikhon's abundant literary legacy (fifteen volumes, strongly revealing the influence of German Pietism) in the early 1860s when he was editing *Time* and beginning to work out his own social-political ideals of *pochvennichestvo* . . . One can find parallels in Tikhon to Father Zosima's adoration of the beauty of nature as a revelation of God's goodness and majesty.'"

55. Gorodetzky, *Saint Tikhon Zadonsky*.

his experience of hearing Scripture read in worship as a child and first truly hears and experiences its power.

> It was a clear day, and, remembering it now, I seem to see again the incense rising from the censer and quietly ascending upwards, and from above, through a narrow window in the cupola, God's rays pouring down upon us in the church, and the incense rising up to them in waves, as if dissolving into them. I looked with deep tenderness, and for the first time in my life I consciously received the first seed of the word of God in my soul. A young man walked out into the middle of the church with a big book, so big that it seemed to me he even had difficulty in carrying it, and he placed it on the analogion, opened it, and began to read, and suddenly, then for the first time I understood something, for the first time in my life I understood what was read in God's church.[56]

His biblically-formed faith is one that resonates with the writing of Hall. Zosima cries out with great affection for Scriptures, "Lord, what a book, what lessons! What a book is the Holy Scripture, what miracle, what power are given to man with it! Like a carven image of the world, and of man, and of human characters, and everything is named and set forth unto ages of ages."[57] The connection between the affections and the longing for beauty expressed in understanding the word is expressed by Zosima: "The people will perish without the word of God, for their souls thirst for his word and for every beautiful perception."[58] It is in this context that the often-quoted phrase of Dostoevsky is to be understood: "Beauty will save the world." This value and evocative use of beauty in the word we see in the pen of Bishop Hall:

> It is not hasty reading, but seriously meditating upon holy and heavenly truths that makes them prove sweet and profitable to the soul. It is not the bee's touching on the flowers that gathers the honey, but her abiding for a time upon them, and drawing out the sweet. It is not he that reads most, but he that meditates most on divine truth, that will prove the choicest, wisest, strongest Christian.[59]

---

56. Dostoevsky, *Brothers Karamazov*, 291.
57. Dostoevsky, *Brothers Karamazov*, 292.
58. Dostoevsky, *Brothers Karamazov*, 294.
59. Hall, *Art*, 103.

Appendix A: Hall's Sources Overview

LOUIS L. MARTZ PROVIDED a landmark study on Bishop Hall in his 1954 work entitled *The Poetry of Meditation*. He argued that both Hall and Ignatius (Hall's Jesuit counterpart) were influenced by Dutch monk Joannes Mauburnus's, work entitled *Scala Meditatoria* (1494).

As a literary scholar with a focus on English literature of the seventeenth century, Martz has reintroduced the key influential role Hall's work on meditation had on the body of literature known as the Metaphysical Poets. He argued that it would be better to call them the Poets of Meditation because of the influence of a practical piety in common with the *Spiritual Exercises* of Loyola.

As a student of Louis Martz, Milo Kaufmann built on the key role that meditative practice had on Bunyan's *Pilgrim's Progress*. Kaufmann sees a discontinuity between some like Hall and the more allegorical approach of Bunyan. These two divergent lines, he proposes, are found in one developed by Hall as a more restrictive method that is less open to the use of the imagination. Bunyan showed another line of practice, which Kaufmann refers to as "imaginative realism," that readily employed the world and the senses as sources of contemplation. These lines of divergence are, arguably, overstated, as this study has affirmed Hall in the same line of using the imagination as a key element of meditation. Kaufmann is another important example of a literary scholar who sheds light on a neglected aspect of Puritan devotional literature that shows the important interplay in the seventeenth century of theology, religious conflict, and the development of modern English literature.

Richard McCabe is in the literary circle of those who have reintroduced Hall's forgotten legacy in English literature on the level of John Donne. The central contribution McCabe makes, for the purpose of this study, is his critique of Kaufmann's view that Hall represented a substantial departure from the imaginative method of the Ignatian tradition and in fact shows common traits and similar examples of the use of occasional and sensory types of contemplation found in the *Spiritual Exercises*. While this does not prove a direct indebtedness of Hall to Ignatius, it does highlight a similar trajectory of source use. This line of continuity is an important argument in the development of a Puritan literature that held a positive role of the imagination.

Secondly, McCabe presents a more careful historical development of Hall's sources and adds a more nuanced and refined view of Hall's indebtedness to a wide spectrum of meditative practices rooted in the *devotio moderna*. He sees little evidence in what Kaufmann sees as Hall's restriction of the imagination. Jean Gerson's influence is noted not just by the three times Hall quotes him in his *Art of Divine Meditation* but by his use of Gerson's allegorical methodology and style. This connection and debt to Gerson has been explored in greater detail.

Finally, it is Frank Huntley's major contribution in his research for two entire books on Hall in a highly detailed way. His survey is both historical and literary and his reach both in style and theological depth presents the reader with an invaluable assessment of Hall's legacy on English Protestant devotional literature—a legacy that needs to be recovered to its rightful place.

Appendix B: Timeline of Bishop Hall

1558 Elizabethan Settlement—Return of Protestant exiles from Europe.
1574 Joseph Hall born July 1 at Bristow Park, Leicestershire.
1583 John Whitgift consecrated archbishop of Canterbury.
1603 Accession of James IV of Scotland after death of Elizabeth I.
1604 Hampton Court Conference; death of Whitgift; Bancroft made archbishop.
1605 Gunpowder Plot conspiracy to blow up the Parliament.
1606 *The Art of Divine Meditation* published.
1610 Death of Archbishop Bancroft.
1611 Authorized Version of the Bible published.
1616 Hall's visit to France—with British ambassador, Doncastere.
1616 Made Dean of Worcester by James.
1618 Synod of Dordt; Thirty Years' War is started.
1630 *Occasional Meditations* is published.
1641 Made Bishop of Norwich and imprisoned.
1647 *Christ Mystical* is published (a favorite of General Gordon).
1652 *The Invisible World* is published.
1652 *The Great Mystery of Godliness laid forth by way of Affections* published.
1656 His death at eighty-seven years old.

Appendix C: Steps of Meditation Illustrated

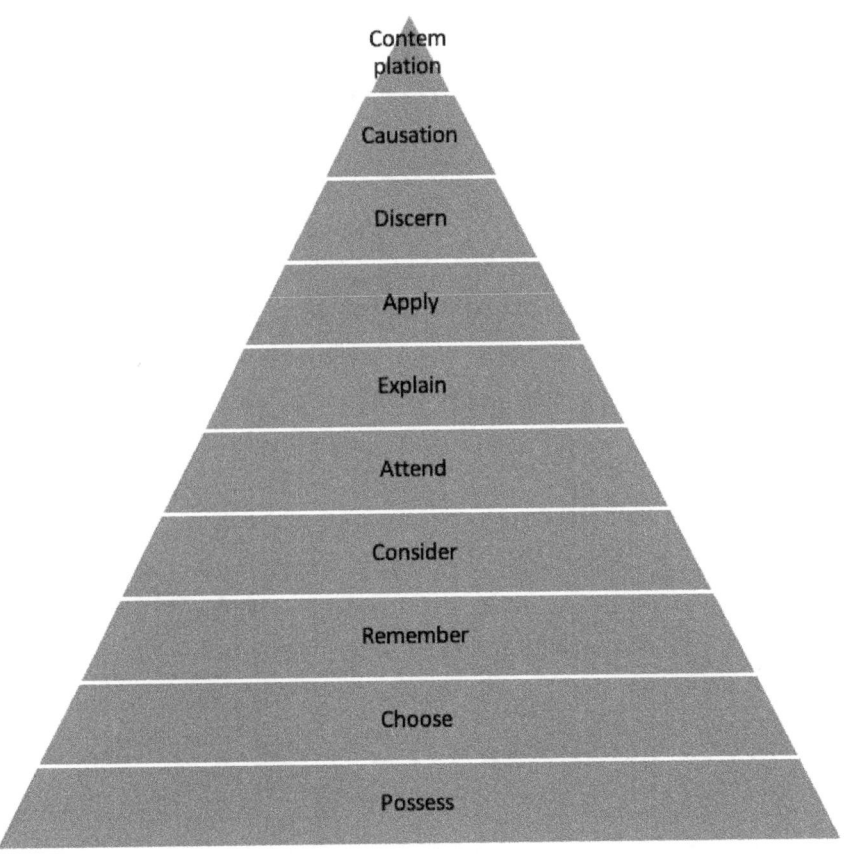

1. Possess—taking hold of what to meditate on.
2. Decide—choosing one thing over others.
3. Remember—recalling from memory truths or thoughts about it.
4. Consider—revolving the mind over the subject.
5. Attend—focusing the mind on one area.
6. Compare—seeking analogies and similar truths.
7. Apply—extending the focus in other areas.
8. Discern—considering the value of the subject above other things.
9. Confirm—confirmation or making it to effect something.
10. Contemplation—"chewing the cud," repeating the steps of meditation until affections are stirred.

THE AFFECTIONS IN MEDITATION—THE DESCENT

1. Requiring a taste and relish of what was thought.
2. Complaint of our lack of desire.
3. A heartfelt wish for the soul to desire what it lacks.
4. Humble confession of one's inability to affect desire.
5. Earnest petition to confess what we lack.
6. A vehement cry of the petition.
7. A cheerful confidence of receiving what we ask.

Bibliography

PRIMARY SOURCES

The Articles of the Synod of Dort, and Its Rejection of Errors: With the History of Events Which Made Way for That Synod, as Published by the Authority of the States-General; and the Documents Confirming Its Decisions. Utica, 1831.

Augustine of Hippo. *The Confessions of St. Augustine, Bishop of Hippo.* London: J. M. Dent, 1950.

―――. "On the Soul and its Origin." In *The Nicene and Post-Nicene Fathers*, edited by Philip Schaff, 5:313-30. Grand Rapids: Eerdmans, 1997.

―――. "On the Trinity." In *The Nicene and Post-Nicene Fathers*, edited by Philip Schaff, 3:214-430. Grand Rapids: Eerdmans, 1988.

Climacus, John. *The Ladder of Divine Ascent.* Classics of Western Spirituality. New York: Paulist Press, 1982.

De Sales, Francis. *Francis de Sales, Jane de Chantal: Letters of Spiritual Direction.* Classics of Western Spirituality. New York: Paulist Press, 1988.

―――. *Introduction to the Devout Life.* New York: Harper & Row, 1966.

Hall, Joseph. *The Art of Meditation.* Jenkintown, PA: Sovereign Grace Publishers, 1960.

―――. *Christ Mystical, or The Blessed Union of Christ and His Members.* London, 1893.

―――. *Contemplations on the Historical Passages of the Old and New Testament.* Morgan, PA: Soli Deo Gloria, 1995.

―――. *Devotions, Sacred Aphorisms and Religious Table Talk: Selected from the Writings of the Eminently Pious and Learned Bishop Hall; to Which Is Prefixed a Brief Memoir of the Author.* London, 1867.

―――. *Extracts from Various Devotional Writings of Joseph Hall, DD. Formerly Bishop of Norwich.* 2nd ed. Birmingham, UK, 1785.

―――. *Fanatick Moderation, Exemplified in Bishop Hall's Hard Measure, as It Was Written by Himself. To Which Is Annex'd, a Specimen of the Unparralell'd Behaviour of the Sectaries, towards Some Others of That Sacred Order. As Likewise, a General Bill of Mortality of the Clergy of the City of London, Who Were Defunct, by Reason of the Contagious Breath of the Pretended Reformers of That City, from the Year 1641, to the Year 1647.* London, 1730.

———. *Peace among Protestants: A Sermon Preached Before the Synod of Dordt in the Year of Our Lord*. London, 1618.

———. *A Selection from the Writings of Joseph Hall: With Observations of Some Specialties in His Life, Written by His Own Hand*. New York: Robert Carter, 1850.

———. *The Shaking of the Olive-Tree. The Remaining Works of That Incomparable Prelate Joseph Hall, DD, Late Lord Bishop of Norwich*. London, 1660.

———. *Solomon's Divine Arts*. Pilgrim Classic Commentaries. Cleveland, OH: Pilgrim Press, 1991.

———. *The Works of Joseph Hall: With Some Account of His Life and Sufferings*. 12 vols. Oxford, 1837.

Hilton, Walter. *The Scale of Perfection*. Westminster, 1908.

Huntley, Frank Livingston. *Bishop Joseph Hall and Protestant Meditation in Seventeenth-Century England: A Study with Texts of The Art of Divine Meditation (1606) and Occasional Meditations (1633)*. Binghamton, NY: Center for Medieval & Early Renaissance Studies, 1981.

Ignatius of Loyola. *Ignatius of Loyola: The Spiritual Exercises and Selected Works*. Classics of Western Spirituality. New York: Paulist Press, 1991.

Perkins, William. *A Treatise of Mans Imaginations Shewing His Naturall Euill Thoughts: His Want of Good Thoughts: The Way to Reforme Them. Framed and Preached by M. Wil. Perkins*. Cambridge, UK, 1607.

Pseudo-Dionysius. *The Complete Works*. Edited by Paul Rorem. New York: Paulist Press, 1987.

Teresa of Avila. *Santa Teresa; an Appreciation, with Some of the Best Passages of the Saint's Writings Selected*. Edinburgh, 1897.

Underhill, Evelyn. *The Cloud of Unknowing: The Classic of Medieval Mysticism*. Mineola, NY: Dover, 2003.

Ussher, James. *A Method for Meditation, or, A Manuall of Divine Duties, Fit for Every Christians Practice*. London, 1651.

SECONDARY SOURCES

Allen, Diogenes. "George Herbert and Simone Weil." *Religion & Literature* 17.2 (1985) 17–34.

Angeles, Peter A. *Dictionary of Philosophy*. New York: Barnes and Noble, 1981.

Bangs, Carl. *Arminius: A Study in the Dutch Reformation*. Nashville: Abingdon, 1971.

Barbee, David M. "A Reformed Catholike: William Perkins' Use of the Church Fathers." PhD diss., University of Pennsylvania, 2013.

Barker, Arthur Edward. *Milton and the Puritan Dilemma, 1641–1660*. Toronto: University of Toronto Press, 1976.

Baucum, Todd D. "Bishop Hall and Ignatius of Loyola: Counter-Reformation Spirituality and the Rise of Protestant Spiritual Methods in Meditation." ThM class paper, Puritan Reformed Theological Seminary, 2017.

Bavinck, Herman. *Essays on Religion, Science, and Society*. Grand Rapids: Baker Academic, 2008.

———. *Reformed Dogmatics*. 4 vols. Grand Rapids: Baker Academic, 2011.

Baxter, Richard. *The Saint's Everlasting Rest*. New York: Robert Carter, 1855.

Beeke, Joel R. "Calvin on Piety." In *The Cambridge Companion to Calvin*, edited by Donald McKim, 125–52. Cambridge, UK: Cambridge University Press, 2004.

———. *Puritan Reformed Spirituality*. Darlington, UK: Evangelical Press, 2006.

Beeke, Joel R., and Mark Jones. *Puritan Theology: Doctrine for Life*. Grand Rapids: Reformation Heritage Books, 2012.

Benedict. *Rule of St. Benedict*. Edited by Timothy Fry. Collegeville, MN: Liturgical Press, 1982.

Beougher, Timothy K. *Richard Baxter and Conversion: A Study of the Puritan Concept of Becoming a Christian*. Scotland: Mentor, 2007.

Bernard of Clairvaux. *Bernard of Clairvaux: Selected Works*. Classics of Western Spirituality. New York: Paulist, 1987.

———. *The Two-Fold Knowledge: Readings on the Knowledge of the Self and the Knowledge of God*. Edited by Franz Posset. Milwaukee, WI: Marquette University Press, 2004.

Blair, Worden. *Literature and Politics in Cromwellian England: John Milton, Andrew Marvell, Marchamont Nedham*. Oxford: Oxford University Press, 2007.

Boersma, Hans. *Seeing God: The Beatific Vision in Christian Tradition*. Grand Rapids: Eerdmans, 2018.

Bouyer, Louis. *History of Christian Spirituality*. New York: Seabury Press, 1982.

Bray, Gerald Lewis. *Documents of the English Reformation 1526–1701*. Cambridge, UK: James Clarke, 2004.

Buckley, Michael J. *At the Origins of Modern Atheism*. New Haven: Yale University Press, 1987.

Bunyan, John. *The Pilgrim's Progress*. Edited by Roger Pooley. Hammondsworth, UK: Penguin, 2008.

Calvin, Jean. *Commentary on Romans*. Grand Rapids: Baker, 1984.

———. *Institutes of the Christian Religion*. Grand Rapids: Eerdmans, 1995.

Canlis, Julie. *Calvin's Ladder: A Spiritual Theology of Ascent and Ascension*. Grand Rapids: Eerdmans, 2010.

Chadwick, Henry. *Augustine: Past Masters*. Oxford: Oxford University Press, 1986.

Chan, Simon. *Spiritual Theology: A Systematic Study of the Christian Life*. Downers Grove: InterVarsity, 1998.

———. "Puritan Meditative Tradition, 1599–1691: A Study of Ascetical Piety." PhD diss., Magdalene College, 1986.

Chang, Curtis. *Engaging Unbelief: A Captivating Strategy from Augustine & Aquinas*. Downers Grove: InterVarsity, 2000.

Coffey, John, ed. *Heart Religion: Evangelical Piety in England and Ireland, 1690–1850*. Oxford: Oxford University Press, 2016.

Cognet, Louis. *Post-Reformation Spirituality*. New York: Hawthorn, 1959.

Cohen, Adam. "Making Memories in a Medieval Miscellany." *Gesta* 48.2 (Jan 2009) 135–52.

Collinson, Patrick. *The Religion of Protestants: The Church in English Society, 1559–1625*. Oxford: Clarendon, 1984.

Collmer, R. G. *Bunyan in Our Time*. Kent, OH: Kent State University Press, 1989.

Connolly, James L. *John Gerson: Reformer and Mystic*. Leuven: Librairie Universitaire, 1928.

Copleston, Frederick C. *Medieval Philosophy*. New York: Harper, 1961.

Corcoran, Kevin J. *Rethinking Human Nature: A Christian Materialist Alternative to the Soul.* Grand Rapids: Baker, 2006.

Corwin, Virginia. *St. Ignatius and Christianity in Antioch.* New Haven: Yale University Press, 1960.

Crawford, James Stewart. "Ignatian Spirituality and the Reformed Tradition: The Use of Spiritual Disciplines in a Presbyterian Congregation." DMin diss., Lancaster Theological Seminary, 2007.

Daniel, Greg K. "The Puritan Ladder of Meditation: An Explication of Puritan Meditation and Its Compatibility with Catholic Meditation." Master's thesis, Trinity Evangelical Divinity School, 1993.

Davis, David J. *Seeing Faith, Printing Pictures: Religious Identity During the English Reformation.* Leiden: Brill, 2013.

Davis, Robert Glenn. "The Force of Union: Affect and Ascent in the Theology of Bonaventure." PhD diss., Harvard University, 2012.

Dever, Mark. *The Affectionate Theology of Richard Sibbes.* Sanford, FL: Reformation Trust, 2018.

Dewar, Michael W. "Bishop Joseph Hall (1574–1656): An Ecumenical Calvinist Churchman." *Churchman* 80.3 (1966) 1–6.

Diehl, John. "From Piety to Parchment: Monastic Spirituality and the Formation of Literate Cultures, 1050–1200." PhD diss., New York University, 2011.

Dostoyesky, Fyodor. *The Brothers Karamazov.* San Francisco: North Press, 1990.

Dupré, Louis, and Don E. Saliers, eds. *Christian Spirituality: Post-Reformation and Modern.* New York: Crossroad, 1990.

Dyrness, William A. *Reformed Theology and Visual Culture: The Protestant Imagination from Calvin to Edwards.* Cambridge, UK: Cambridge University Press, 2004.

Edwards, Jonathan. *The Religious Affections.* Edinburgh: Banner of Truth, 2004.

Elder, E. Rozanne, ed. *The Roots of the Modern Christian Tradition.* Kalamazoo, MI: Cistercian Publications, 1984.

Engelsma, David. *Always Reforming: Continuation of the Sixteenth-Century Reformation.* Jenison, MI: Reformed Free Publishing Association, 2009.

Ford, Alan. *James Ussher: Theology, History, and Politics in Early-Modern Ireland and England.* Oxford: Oxford University Press, 2007.

Frank, Joseph. *Dostoevsky: The Mantle of a Prophet, 1871–1881.* Princeton: Princeton University Press, 2002.

Fuller, Edmund. *John Milton.* London: Gollancz, 1969.

Fuller, Thomas. *The History of the Worthies of England.* London, 1662.

Gamble, Richard C. *Articles on Calvin and Calvinism: A Fourteen-Volume Anthology of Scholarly Articles.* New York: Garland, 1992.

Gilson, Etienne. *The Philosophy of St. Bonaventure.* New York: St. Anthony Guild Press, 1965.

Gorodetzky, Nadejda. *Saint Tikhon Zadonsky: Inspirer of Dostoevsky.* London: SPCK, 1951.

Goudriaan, Aza, and F. A. van Lieburg. *Revisiting the Synod of Dordt (1618–1619).* Leiden: Brill, 2011.

Greef, W. de. *The Writings of John Calvin: An Introductory Guide.* Louisville: Westminster John Knox, 2008.

Green, I. M. *Print and Protestantism in Early Modern England.* Oxford: Oxford University Press, 2000.

Gunton, Colin E. *Father, Son, and Holy Spirit: Essays Toward a Fully Trinitarian Theology*. London: T. & T. Clark, 2003.
Hackel, Sergei. "Russian." In *The Study of Spirituality*, edited by Cheslyn Jones et al., 259–76. Oxford: Oxford University Press, 1986.
Hambrick-Stowe, Charles E. *Practice of Piety: Puritan Devotional Disciplines in Seventeenth-Century New England*. Chapel Hill: University of North Carolina Press, 1985.
Hanford, James Holly. *John Milton, Englishman*. New York: Crown Publishers, 1949.
Hanson, Bradley. *Modern Christian Spirituality: Methodological and Historical Essays*. Atlanta: Scholars Press, 1990.
Hasche-Burger, Ulrike. "Music and Meditation: Songs in Johannes Mauburnus's 'Rosetum Exercitorium Spiritualium.'" *Church History and Religious Culture* 88.3 (Jan 2008) 347–69.
Hervey, James. *Meditations and Contemplations*. Vol. 1. London, 1796.
Hill, Christopher. *God's Englishman: Oliver Cromwell and the English Revolution*. New York: Harper & Row, 1972.
Hobbins, Daniel Bruce. "Beyond the Schools: New Writings and the Social Imagination of Jean Gerson." PhD diss., University of Notre Dame, 2002.
Hughes, Philip Edgcumbe. *Lefèvre: Pioneer of Ecclesiastical Renewal in France*. Grand Rapids: Eerdmans, 1984.
Huntley, Frank Livingston. *Bishop Joseph Hall, 1574–1656: A Biographical and Critical Study*. Cambridge, UK: Brewer, 1979.
Joad, Raymond. *Milton's Angels: The Early-Modern Imagination*. Oxford: Oxford University Press, 2010.
Jordan, Richard Douglas. "Thomas Traherne and the Art of Meditation." *Journal of the History of Ideas* 46.3 (1985) 381–403.
Kalthoff, Mark. "The Bohemian Tory and the Oxbridge Knights." *The Imaginative Conservative*, November 2, 2013. https://theimaginativeconservative.org/2013/11/sir-thomas-browne-russell-kirk.html.
Kaufmann, U. Milo. *The Pilgrim's Progress and Traditions in Puritan Meditation*. New Haven: Yale University Press, 1966.
Keeble, N. H. "C. S. Lewis, Richard Baxter, and 'Mere Christianity.'" *Christianity & Literature* 30.3 (June 1981) 27–44.
Kinloch, T. F. *The Life and Works of Joseph Hall, 1574–1656*. London: Staples, 1951.
Knowles, David. *The English Mystical Tradition*. New York: Harper, 1961.
Kolk, Bessel van der. *The Body Keeps Score: Brain, Mind, and Body in the Healing of Trauma*. New York: Penguin, 2015.
Kommattam, Flower. "John Donne's 'Devotions Upon Emergent Occasions' and Traditions of Meditation." PhD diss., University of Toronto, 1993.
Lake, Peter. "The Laudian Style: Order, Uniformity and the Pursuit of the Beauty of Holiness in the 1630s." In *The Early Stuart Church, 1603–1642*, edited by Kenneth Fincham, 161–87. Basingstoke, UK: Macmillan, 1993.
Lane, Belden C. *Landscapes of the Sacred: Geography and Narrative in American Spirituality*. New York: Paulist Press, 1988.
———. *Ravished by Beauty: The Surprising Legacy of Reformed Spirituality*. Oxford: Oxford University Press, 2011.

Lashier, Jackson. "The Mediated and Undiluted Light: Hierarchy, Mediation, and the Vision of God in the Works of Dionysius Areopagatica." *Greek Orthodox Theological Review* 51.1–4 (Spring 2006) 45–70.

Leclercq, Jean. *The Love of Learning and Desire for God: A Study of Monastic Culture.* New York: Fordham University Press, 1982.

Leeuwen, Theodoor Marius van, et al. *Arminius, Arminianism, and Europe: Jacobus Arminius (1559/60–1609).* Leiden: Brill, 2009.

Lewis, C. S. *God in the Dock: Essays on Theology and Ethics.* Grand Rapids: Eerdmans, 1970.

———. *Selected Literary Essays.* Cambridge, UK: Cambridge University Press, 1969.

———. *Till We Have Faces.* New York: Harcourt, 1984.

Lindberg, Carter. *The European Reformations.* Malden, MA: Wiley-Blackwell, 2010.

Luxon, Thomas H. *Literal Figures: Puritan Allegory and the Reformation Crisis in Representation.* Chicago: University of Chicago Press, 1995.

MacCulloch, Diarmaid. *All Things Made New: The Reformation and Its Legacy.* Oxford: Oxford University Press, 2016.

Martz, Louis L. "Meditation." In *Seventeenth Century Prose and Poetry*, edited by Alexander Witherspoon and Frank J. Warnke, 1082–93. New York: Harcourt Brace Javanovich, 1982.

———. *The Poetry of Meditation: A Study in English Religious Literature of the Seventeenth Century.* New Haven: Yale University Press, 1954.

Mayfield, Sandra J. "The Influence of the Art of Mediation on Sir Thomas Browne's Imagination." PhD diss., University of Oklahoma Press, 1980.

McCabe, Richard A. *Joseph Hall: A Study in Satire and Meditation.* Oxford: Oxford University Press, 1982.

McGinn, Bernard, John Meyendorff, and Jean Leclercq. *Christian Spirituality.* New York: Crossroad, 1985.

Medwick, Cathleen. *Teresa of Avila: The Progress of a Soul.* New York: Knopf, 1999.

Merton, Thomas. *Bread in the Wilderness.* Collegeville, MN: Liturgical Press, 1986.

Milosh, Joseph E. *The Scale of Perfection and the English Mystical Tradition.* Madison: University of Wisconsin Press, 1996.

Milton, Anthony. *Catholic and Reformed: The Roman and Protestant Churches in English Protestant Thought, 1600–1640.* Cambridge, UK: Cambridge University Press, 2002.

———, et al., eds. *The Oxford History of Anglicanism.* Oxford: Oxford University Press, 2017.

Moorman, John R. H. *The Anglican Spiritual Tradition.* Springfield, IL: Templegate Publishers, 1983.

Moser, Christian., H. J. Selderhuis, and Donald W. Sinnema, eds. *Acta of the Synod of Dordt (1618–1619).* Göttingen: Vandenhoeck & Ruprecht, 2014.

Muller, Richard A. *After Calvin: Studies in the Development of a Theological Tradition.* Oxford: Oxford University Press, 2003.

———. *Dictionary of Latin and Greek Theological Terms: Drawn Principally from Protestant Scholastic Theology.* Grand Rapids: Baker Academic, 2017.

———. *Divine Will and Human Choice: Freedom, Contingency, and Necessity in Early Modern Reformed Thought.* Grand Rapids: Baker Academic, 2017.

———. *Post-Reformation Reformed Dogmatics: The Rise and Development of Reformed Orthodoxy, ca. 1520 to ca. 1725.* Grand Rapids: Baker Academics, 2003.

Newey, Vincent. *The Pilgrim's Progress: Critical and Historical Views.* Liverpool: Liverpool University Press, 1980.
Oberman, Heiko A. *The Dawn of the Reformation: Essays in Late Medieval and Early Reformation Thought.* Edinburgh: T. & T. Clark, 1986.
———. *The Harvest of Medieval Theology: Gabriel Biel and Late Medieval Nominalism.* Durham, NC: Labyrinth Press, 1983.
Owen, H. P. "Christian Mysticism: A Study in Walter Hilton's 'The Ladder of Perfection.'" *Religious Studies* 7.1 (1971) 31–42.
Ozment, Steven E. *The Age of Reform (1250–1550): An Intellectual and Religious History of Late Medieval and Reformation Europe.* New Haven: Yale University Press, 1980.
Packer, J. I. *A Quest for Godliness: The Puritan Vision of the Christian Life.* Wheaton: Crossway Books, 1990.
Patterson, W. B. *King James VI and I and the Reunion of Christendom.* Cambridge, UK: Cambridge University Press, 2000.
Pederson, Randall J. *Unity in Diversity: English Puritans and the Puritan Reformation, 1603–1689.* Leiden: Brill, 2014.
Pino, Tikhon Alexander. "Continuity in Patristic and Scholastic Thought: Bonaventure and Maximos the Confessor on the Necessary Multiplicity of God." *Franciscan Studies* 72 (2014) 107–28.
Price, J. L. *Dutch Culture in the Golden Age.* London: Reaktion Books, 2011.
Rapley, Elizabeth. *The Lord Is Their Portion: The Story of the Religious Orders and How They Shaped the World.* Grand Rapids: Eerdmans, 2011.
Reuver, Arie de. *Sweet Communion: Trajectories of Spirituality from the Middle Ages through the Further Reformation.* Grand Rapids: Baker Academic, 2007.
Rice, Howard. *Reformed Spirituality.* Louisville: Westminster John Knox, 1991.
Riehle, Wolfgang. *The Middle English Mystics.* London: Routledge & Kegan Paul, 1981.
Rowe, Karen E. "Sacred or Profane?: Edward Taylor's Meditations on Canticles." *Modern Philology* 72.2 (1974) 123–38.
Ryrie, Alec, and Tom Schwanda, eds. *Puritanism and Emotion in the Early Modern World.* Basingstoke, UK: Palgrave Macmillan, 2016.
Saxton, David W. *God's Battle Plan for the Mind: The Puritan Practice of Biblical Meditation.* Master's thesis, Puritan Reformed Theological Seminary, 2013.
Schwanda, Tom. "Saints' Desire and Delight to Be with Christ." In *Puritanism and Emotion in the Early Modern World*, edited by Alec Ryrie and Tom Schwanda, 70–93. New York: Springer Press, 2016.
———. *Soul Recreation: The Contemplative-Mystical Piety of Puritanism.* Eugene, OR: Pickwick, 2012.
———. "Sweetness in Communion with God: The Contemplative-Mystical Piety of Thomas Watson." *Journal of the History of Reformed Pietism* 1.2 (2015) 34–63.
Senn, Frank. *Protestant Spiritual Traditions.* New York: Paulist Press, 1986.
Shaw, Ian. *Churches, Revolutions, and Empires (1789–1914).* Fearn, UK: Christian Focus, 2012.
Sheldrake, Philip. *Heaven in Ordinary: George Herbert and His Writings.* Norwich, UK: Canterbury Press, 2009.
Sibbes, Richard. *Soul's Conflict.* Philadelphia: Presbyterian Board of Publication, 1842.
Simon, Chan. *The Puritan Meditative Tradition, 1599–1691: A Study of Ascetical Piety.* PhD diss., Magdalene College, 1986.
Smith, Philip A. "Bishop Hall: 'Our English Seneca.'" *PMLA* 63.4 (1948) 1191–1204.

Sommerfeldt, John R. *Bernard of Clairvaux on the Spirituality of Relationship*. New York: Newman, 2004.

Spurr, John. *The Post-Reformation: Religion, Politics and Society in Britain, 1603–1714*. New York: Pearson Longman, 2006.

———. *The Restoration Church of England, 1646–1689*. New Haven: Yale University Press, 1991.

Steere, Daniel J. "'For the Peace of Both, for the Humour of Neither': Bishop Joseph Hall Defends the Via Media in an Age of Extremes, 1601–1656." *The Sixteenth Century Journal* 27.3 (1996) 749–65.

———. "Quo Vadis?: Bishop Joseph Hall and the Demise of the Calvinist Conformity in Early Seventeenth-Century England." PhD diss., Georgia State University, 2000.

Stott, John. *Balanced Christianity*. Downers Grove, IL: InterVarsity Press, 1975.

Stranks, C. J. *Anglican Devotion: Studies in the Spiritual Life of the Church of England Between the Reformation and the Oxford Movement*. London: SCM Press, 1961.

Stutfield, Hugh E. M. *Mysticism and Catholicism*. London: Unwin, 1925.

Tamburello, Dennis E. *Union with Christ: John Calvin and the Mysticism of St. Bernard*. Louisville: Westminster John Knox, 1994.

Thiselton, Anthony. *Thiselton Companion to Christian Theology*. Grand Rapids: Eerdmans, 2015.

Thornton, Martin. "The Caroline Divines and the Cambridge Platonists." In *The Study of Spirituality*, edited by Cheslyn Jones et al., 431–37. Oxford: Oxford University Press, 1986.

Toon, Peter. *From Mind to Heart: Christian Meditation Today*. Grand Rapids: Baker Book House, 1987.

———. *Meditating as a Christian*. London: Collins, 1991.

———. *Puritans and Calvinism*. Swengel, PA: Reiner, 1973.

Ussher, James. *A Body of Divinity: The Sum and and Substance of Christian Religion*. Birmingham, AL: Solid Ground Christian Books, 2007.

Visser, A. S. Q. *Reading Augustine in the Reformation: The Flexibility of Intellectual Authority in Europe, 1500–1620*. Oxford: Oxford University Press, 2011.

Wands, John Miller. *Another World and Yet the Same: Bishop Joseph Hall's Mundus alter et idem*. New Haven: Yale University Press, 1981.

Watson, Thomas. *The Christian on the Mount: A Treatise on Meditation Wherein the Necessity, and Excellency of Meditation Are Discussed*. Orlando, FL: Northampton, 2009.

Whyte, Alexander. *Santa Teresa: An Appreciation*. Edinburgh: Oliphant, Anderson & Ferrer, 1898.

William of St. Thierry. *On Contemplating God*. Translated by Geoffrey Webb and Adrian Walker. Riverside, IL: Akenside Press, 2017.

William, Marceau. *The Notion of the Eucharist in Théodore de Bèze and St. François de Sales*. Master's thesis, University of St. Michael's College, 1991.

Winslow, Ola Elizabeth. *Jonathan Edwards, 1703–1758*. New York: Collier Books, 1961.

Zaleski, Philip, and Carol Zaleski. *The Fellowship: The Literary Lives of the Inklings: J. R. R. Tolkien, C. S. Lewis, Owen Barfield, Charles Williams*. New York: Farrar, Straus, and Giroux, 2016.

www.ingramcontent.com/pod-product-compliance
Lightning Source LLC
Chambersburg PA
CBHW051108160426
43193CB00010B/1368